DON'T LEAVE THE NEIGHBOR OUT OF THE HOOD

To: Nikki
Good to Make A New
by *FRIEND.*

Jaime M. Kowlessar

FROM:
DR. J. Kowlessar

Watersprings
PUBLISHING

DON'T LEAVE THE NEIGHBOR OUT OF THE HOOD

Published by Watersprings Media House, LLC.
P.O. Box 1284
Olive Branch, MS 38654
For bulk orders or permission requests contact
publisher. www.waterspringsmedia.com

ISBN 13: 978-1-948877-19-0
ISBN 10: 1-948877-19-8

TABLE OF CONTENTS

THE FORMULA

Resist, Redeem, Reclaim, Renew...

ACKNOWLEDGMENTS

I have been blessed by God to have certain individuals in my life who have inspired me and challenged me to be a better person. First and foremost I would like to acknowledge my Lord and Savior Jesus Christ   and my parents Michael and Lynette Kowlessar for raising me and shaping me into the man that I am today I would also like to acknowledge Dr.' Lester McCorn, Dr. Jamison Hunter, and Dr. Anthony Ledonne for pushing me during every intensive to keep reading and writing; my cohorts in the Gardner Taylor Scholars group, especially Charles Tyler, Kenneth York, and Doug Purcell, (We walked in together, and we will leave together) the wonderful church known as City Temple located in Dallas, Texas for being patient with me, and praying with me during this process, Elder Paul Blocker, Jr., and Uneeda Burgess whose input has been very helpful in my preparation.

Last but definitely not least, I would like to thank Dr. Dedrick Blue and Pastor Eddie Polite. Dr. Blue, you taught me that social justice and Adventism go hand in hand. Pastor Polite, you continued to water the seed that was planted in me by showing me how to implement and carry out the vision of making the world better for others.

I would like to dedicate this project to my lovely wife and two daughters. Carlene, you have toiled with me all night and have pushed me to complete this process when I wanted to give up so many times. Thank you for being a source of strength and a shoulder to lean on. To my beautiful daughters Katelynn and Amber, I thank you for understanding and being patient with daddy as he had to sacrifice some time during the week to study in the local library and take trips out of town for classes and research. This document is to show you that you can do anything that you put your mind to and climb to the highest height. Last but definitely not least, I would like to thank my Lord and Savior Jesus Christ for the strength to make it this far and allowing me to accomplish one of my many goals. I can only imagine where You are going to take me after this, but I am open for the journey.

THE GOSPEL

"There is no whole gospel without compassion and justice shown to the poor. It's that simple."

Richard Stearns

INTRODUCTION

From Genesis to Revelation the Bible is written with the theme of oppression and liberation. The Scriptures constantly remind us that God has always been a strong Redeemer for Israel. Whether they were in Egyptian bondage, Babylonian, or Roman bondage, Israel has always found itself in an unfortunate circumstance needing assistance from a power that is higher than they. The theme of oppression, liberation, and social justice that is found in the Scriptures has been eliminated from many of the pulpits and theologies in the Seventh-day Adventist (SDA) denomination.

For the four years that I have had the opportunity to be the associate minister and now the senior pastor of this wonderful church, it has forced me to grow. Prior to pastoring in Dallas, Texas I served in New York City at the Ephesus SDA Church in Harlem and the Bethany SDA Church in Westbury, Long Island. At least ten years of experience as a full-time Adventist minister have also provided me the platform to visit churches across the country and the world. My observations have revealed that most Seventh-day Adventist churches have the same identity. They are weak in the area of social justice and ministries that relieve the poor and counter oppression. What they are strong in is prophetic messages that address eschatological events, ministries that are charity focused, and a lack of real presence in their communities. I likened my context as a microcosm of the void that is found in so many Adventist churches. I've also discovered that this phenomenon is not only akin to the Seventh-day Adventist church, but this type of thinking prevails in many different congregations. In living in Dallas, I can probably count on one hand in regards to how many churches are preaching and teaching social justice and human rights from the sacred text.

Since Seventh-day Adventists trump themselves as a Bible-based church that adheres to the full Ten Commandments found in Exodus, especially the Fourth Commandment, which admonishes to uphold, upkeep, and observe the Sabbath. The questions that I had to ask and seek an answer are: How was the scope of social justice left out of the Sabbath message? Where did it all begin, and how can it end? Is it a possibility that, because young

Seventh-day Adventist ministers do not receive any type of social justice training on a collegiate or masters level, that it has created a certain identity in Adventist congregations?

Although I have grown up as a lifelong Seventh-day Adventist, served as a deacon, elder, and now a fulltime pastor, I have attempted to write this project as someone from the outside looking in. As an investigator I tried to leave no stone unturned, in my attempt to understand the education or miseducation of the Seventh-day Adventists as it relates to social justice.

Throughout this book you will also discover that social justice is not something that is a new concept or idea for the church. Instead, you will see that it is something that we have strayed away from. The early pioneers that started the denomination were actively engaged in fighting for the rights of the slaves in the antebellum South. During the Civil Rights Movement many black ministers were engaged on the spiritual and local levels for their own rights and the rights of others. Within the book it is important to note that the term blacks and African Americans are used synonymously.

The first chapter of this document deals with the context in which I am planted in as a Seventh-day Adventist, with the unique challenges that the Seventh day Adventists face in the community, and with themselves. Most black SDA churches are located in impoverished areas; some of them are affluent churches that have not made any real impact in their neighborhoods.

In chapter two I attempt to address the issue with the biblical examples of Nehemiah and Jesus. Nehemiah lives in the palace, but he is devastated by the destruction of the walls in Jerusalem, so he leaves the palace to build. Jesus, who was born in Nazareth, returns home to the temple to stand up and read a message of social justice and hope.

I use the third chapter, historical foundations, to travel back historically into the archives of Adventism. I am particularly looking at black Adventist ministers and members who were actively engaged in social justice. The focus of the chapter is to prove the thesis that not all Adventists are apathetic towards social involvement and the uplifting work that the sacred text class us to do.

Chapter four compares Adventist Theology with that of James Cone's black liberation theology, and Jürgen Moltmann's theology of hope. Adventists pride themselves on being Sabbath keepers, but in their Sabbath keeping they have overlooked the liberating nature of the commandment. Chapter five pays careful attention to the factors that lead to what is commonly known as the 'hood' or the 'ghetto.' Gentrification, redlining, redistribution, and economic justice are some of the topics were discussed.

Chapter five of the book concentrates on the solution to the problem and the results as well a general overview of my thoughts and reactions throughout the process.

Chapter six will be used for developing a framework for churches of all denominations to use if they are desirous of establishing a sustainable and viable social justice ministry.

This project has been a journey for me in trying to reverse and renew a thinking that has been long forgotten amongst our members. This book is for that pastor or church scholar that is in the middle of a food desert, crime, and lack of proper infrastructure and resources. What is their answer? and How will they accomplish it in this community, especially in the times that we are living in?

We are living in defining moments in the history of the United States of America. We have elected our first African-American President who has served for two terms. Just recently we elected Donald Trump to be our President for the next four years. He is an individual who has no political experience in his life but has made billions by erecting and dismantling buildings. He is an individual who has made his political claim to fame by questioning the legitimacy of Barak Obama's birth certificate. In between all of that, we have witnessed the untimely deaths of so many unarmed African Americans: Trayvon Martin, Eric Garner, Walter Scott, Jordan Davis, Michael Brown, Tamir Ryce, Philando Castille, Rekia Boyd, Sandra Blanc, Danroy Henry, and the Charlotte Nine are just to name a few. As the Smithsonian opened the African-American Museum as well as in Washington, D.C., they unveiled the Martin Luther

King, Jr., Memorial; we are still at a crossroad when it comes to social sacrificial justice, equality, and basic human rights. These answers and many more questions will arise in this book; I hope that you are intrigued, satisfied, and challenged to expect more and to do more. I hope that you will help me put the neighbor, back in the hood.

THE CONTEXT

1

I have resided in Texas for about five years. I moved here to accept a call to be the youth and young adult pastor of a prominent church. I've always had a passion for youth and young adults, but a shift began to take place during my seventh year of ministry. While I was pastoring in New York City, I can vividly remember a Wednesday night when, one of my members was standing up and asking the church to pray for her son because he was not doing so well in school. She went on to describe the conditions in the school the paint was chipping, the textbooks were old, and the building could use a makeover. After she gave that heartfelt stirring testimony, everyone in the congregation declared boldly that they would pray for her. I remember getting up after she gave that testimony to give the devotional thought for that evening. Whilst I was speaking, I just kept hearing her words running through my brain about the conditions of her son's school and his failing grades. As I drove home that evening, I could not stop thinking about all the things that were said that evening, and the fact that the only response the church had to this woman's plight was, "We will pray for you." Forget about the church; I was bothered by the fact that it was my only response, and I proceeded to preach about nothing that had to do with what she said. I was bothered so much by the fact that my sermons did not address any of the issues that my congregants were dealing with from day to day. I was bothered by the fact that all we knew how to do for each other is pray. Now, I know that someone is reading this and you're probably saying to yourself, "What's wrong with prayer?!?" For the record let it be known that there is nothing wrong with praying, but there is something obviously wrong with us just saying that we will pray for someone without at least seeking ways to fix the problem not only for them but for others. I thought about the other kids who have to sit in dropout factories across my city. There has to be more! We can do more than just pray.

Since then, I began to include more instances of social justice in my sermons. I started to empower individuals to be more vocal about the things that they despise, or the things that intentionally hurt them from a societal standpoint. It has opened a lot of doors for me and has put me in a lot of spaces with others who are trying to do the work of justice from a faith and a nonreligious background. That was 2007; fast forward to 2013, and now I have a call from Texas to come and pastor in this strange land. I didn't want any part of it because I was born and raised in New York City, and, as a New Yorker, I never thought or could see myself living anywhere other than in the concrete jungle of Brooklyn, NY. To make a long story short, my wife and I decided to pack up our family and live in Texas. A major part of my moving was to also see what life and ministry was like outside of New York City.

I must admit that New York and Texas are polar opposites in regards to look, feel, and even smell. Poverty in Texas is more explicit and blatant. You could see in front of your face how there are certain businesses set up to keep poor people poor. Car title loan advance shops, check cashing shops, pawn shops, and liquor stores are everywhere you turn. Texas has one of the biggest grocery gaps in America. There are little to no areas where residents can obtain fresh fruits and vegetables. At least in New York mass transit provides an opportunity for individuals to get around; in Texas those things are far and wide.

To most Texans in poor communities they are prisoners in their own neighborhoods. If you do not have a vehicle, then chances are you have to buy groceries from a local bodega. It's absolutely amazing that a person's zip code can determine how long they will live. The reality is that if you live in an impoverished community, it will determine the kind of education you will receive, what hospital you will get driven too, as well as the services in your neighborhood. Studies have shown that the poor are targeted by the police in certain neighbors, arrested, and mandated by the court to pay high bonds for their freedom. Some communities look like third world countries. The children are forced to play in areas that are drug infested with bullet casings on the ground. In the midst of all of that, there will be a church. In some cases that church will have its door closed all week and only open up for worship. We have become in some cases okay with having grade "A" worship in grade "F" communities.

In the midst of all of that, the church appears to be apathetic towards ministries of social justice and trying to alleviate the pain of those that are hurting both physically and spiritually. However, the display towards social justice is more of an appearance than an actuality. While conducting research, it has become clear that the congregation has a blind spot for the needs of the community.

One of the defining pillars of the Seventh-day Adventist Church is found in its name. Seventh-day Adventists are a Protestant sect that believes in the imminent return of Jesus Christ, and observes Saturday as the Sabbath, based upon the Fourth Commandment found in Exodus 20:8-11. The body holds twenty-eight fundamental beliefs which range from The Trinity, State of the Dead, Spiritual Gifts, the Apocalypse, and many more. In the midst of all the teachings, doctrines, and twenty-eight fundamental beliefs, there is no response to social injustice, political activism, or consciousness towards those that are oppressed. The headquarters of the Seventh-day Adventist church is in Silver Spring, Maryland; the denomination has churches in almost every part of the world, according to their website,

The church is served through its administration of thirteen world divisions and two attached fields. No matter where you are, you will find a Seventh-day Adventist believer; you will find them adhering to the ideals described by the Bible. Their lives will illustrate both faith in God and the church's commitment to the betterment of all human beings.

The thirteen world divisions and two attached fields consist of East-Central Africa, Euro-Asia, Middle East and North Africa, Inter-American, Inter-European, Israel Field, Northern Asia-Pacific, Southern Africa-Indian Ocean, South American, South Pacific, Southern Asia, Southern Asia-Pacific, Trans-European, West-Central Africa, and the North American Division.

One of the unique elements of the Seventh-day Adventist Church is that it is broken down in layers. The General Conference is at the top, and this is known as the headquarters. Underneath the General Conference fall the thirteen divisions. The thirteen divisions oversee the work of the local unions. The unions oversee the work of the various conferences that are strategically placed across the globe. The various Seventh-day conferences

manage and oversee the work pertaining to the local churches. Each layer has its own governing body consisting of a President, Secretary (Vice President), and Treasurer. It is important to note that the Seventh-day Adventist Church also has disaster relief organizations, hospitals, and the second largest parochial school system in the world. The Adventist churches in America fall under the North American Division, which covers the Southwest Union, which oversees the Southwest Regional
Conference.

The People's Praise Empowerment Center SDA Church is ninety-five years old. It was established in the summer of 1919 from a small tent meeting that was pitched on Central Avenue in Dallas. This small tent resulted in the first congregation, which only consisted of twenty-five members. The church has seen many ups and downs and various relocations. In 1923, the church moved from gathering inside of a member's home to a building. By the year 1950, the membership of the church was the largest it had ever been. In 1956, it adopted the name The People's Praise

Empowerment Center as its official name. It was during the year of 1956 that active ministries were formulated.

A community service project for a nursery, kindergarten and preschool program cared for 120 children daily. An active welfare program cared for the needs of the disadvantaged and indigent in the local community.

On May 16, 1971, the church relocated once again to its current location. In regards to this move, a startling comment was made by one of the members:

The opinion continued that the climate around the church also changed. The move to Oak Cliff occurred around the Civil Rights movement that brought integration, so now we, as a Black people, could do things we could not do before. The church was no longer the center of activity. We had other choices; we could now go more places. The culture of the Black family also changed with the Civil Rights movement. Now blacks were becoming doctors and lawyers and administrators and teachers.

The statement jolts me because I do not believe that this is unique to just P.P.E.C (People's Praise and Empowerment Center), but I believe that this expresses the beliefs of many other black churches in North America. The part of the quote that stood out to me was, "the church was no longer the center of activity." There has developed this languor and surrendering of social justice issues by the black church. Since its inception, P.P.E.C has had twenty-six different pastors. The church has seen its ups and downs.

I strongly believe that the reason the church is not currently involved in an active social justice ministry is because Adventist Theology does not support, teach, or train its pastors in that area. In my summation I believe that if ministers are not taught to interpret the Scriptures through the lens of social injustice, then they cannot relay that message to the congregation. I cannot fault the congregation for lacking in that area. Adventist ministers are encouraged to attend Seventhday Adventist schools for theological training. The issue with this is that our theology is very Eurocentric and caters to a docile and passive listener.

After all, the Adventist denomination came into existence after the Great Disappointment in 1844. William Miller had a faulty mathematical theology that predicted that Jesus would return on October 22, 1844. Out of the disappointment the Adventist denomination grew. The champions of our faith are Joseph Bates, James White, Ellen G. White, and J. N. Andrews. All of them were WASPS (White Anglo-Saxon Protestants). In their eyes, the only threat they deemed as detrimental to them was losing their religious liberty-- their right to worship on Saturday. Very much like the puritans, settlers, and pilgrims, their only threat in life was being persecuted because of their religious beliefs. The founding fathers of our church have never had to worry about crosses being burned on their lawns, witnessing their family members hung on trees, or being born slaves. Although it is a proven fact that in her later years, Ellen G. White commissioned the church to minister to the Negro in the South; it still never took away from the fact that the sole purpose of the church is to protect the Seventh-day Sabbath Commandment. Though things have changed in recent years, the body (denomination) does not sponsor oppression through public policy.

While I was doing the work for Doctor of Ministry at United Theological Seminary in Dayton, OH, I was embarrassed to say that throughout my undergraduate and graduate studies, I was never encouraged to read the writings of Howard Thurman, James Cone, Martin Luther King, Jr., Samuel Dewitt Proctor, Gardner Taylor, W.E.B. Dubois, Frederick Douglass, and the list goes on. Instead, we read commentaries and books that were written from an imperialistic viewpoint. We have done exactly what Forrest E. Harris describes in his book, Ministry for Social Crisis:

"We have not loved God or our neighbors as we ought. We have been bloated with our own conceit, blind to the needs of the Samaritan lying by the side of the road, and corrupted by our desire for power, fame, and personal gain."

The P.P.E.C SDA Church is located in the East Oak Cliff area of Dallas, TX. It is important to note that Texas is one of the fastest-growing states in America. The cover of the October 2013 issue of Time Magazine reads, "The United States of Texas: Why the Lone Star

State is America's Future." The author of the article, Tyler Cowen, lists several reasons to justify his thesis. He states that, "Texas is one of the fastest-growing states, with three of the top five fastest-growing cities in the country: Austin, Dallas and Houston." He claims that people are attracted to the cheaper living, no state-tax, and the fact that there are jobs in Texas. "In the past 12 months, Texas has added 274,700 new jobs — that's 12% of all jobs added nationwide and 51,000 more than California added ... In fact, from 2002 to 2011, with 8% of the U.S. population, Texas created nearly one-third of the country's highest-paying jobs." One of the benefits of cheaper living is that low-income households can survive a lot easier in Texas than in most other states. Another benefit that some people claim is that individuals are opting for a much warmer climate. They would prefer a calendar year with a greater number of warmer months than colder months. In recent years, there has been a major migration from the North to the South. Atlanta is becoming oversaturated with too many people. Young families are looking for somewhere to live where their money can stretch, and the quality of life appears to be better. As a person who was born and raised in New York City, Texas was very inviting because the so-called American Dream appeared to be a reality there. I felt that Texas would present the best opportunity in which to purchase a home with a picket fence and a two-car garage.

Texas appears to be a wonderful state to move to – and do not get me wrong, it is –yet, there is still another side to the coin that we must analyze. According to an article written in the Dallas News business section, Mitchell Schnurman exposes the economic inequality in Texas. He claims that Texas is what appears to be a proud leader in income inequality and wealth distribution. According to Schnurman, however, the gap between the wealthy and the poor is wide. Texas enjoys its land full of oil and barbecue, but in 2010, the poverty rate in Texas was 14.4%. The rate dropped to 10.8% for non-Hispanic whites but soared to 17.1% for blacks and 24.8% for Hispanics, according to the Census Bureau. On January 29, 2014, Steve Campbell wrote an article entitled "A Growing Divide Between Rich and Poor in Texas." He states,

"When you look at poverty rates for African Americans and Hispanics, they are two or three times as high as they are for non-Hispanic whites. Blacks and Hispanic incomes are 60 to 75 percent compared to whites."

Therefore, African Americans and Hispanics continue to struggle as their counterparts seem to be doing well. As the rich get richer, the poor get poorer; it has become the land of the "have gots" and "the have nots."

In addition to a considerable gap in regards to economic equality, Texas finds itself as one of the states that incarcerates black and brown people at very disturbing rates. According to a document published by the Justice Policy Institute:

African Americans are incarcerated at 5 times the rate of Whites in Texas (3,734 per 100,000, compared to 694 per 100,000 Whites). There are more African American men of all ages in prison in Texas (66,300) than in the higher education system (40,800). A national report published by JPI in August 2003 showed that nearly twice as many African Americans [sic] men in their early 30s have prison records (22%) than Bachelors degrees (12%). The number for Hispanics is staggering as well:

In 2002, Latinos were a greater share of new prison admissions than either African Americans or

Whites (33.9% Latinos, 32.8% African Americans, and 32.7% Whites). Conversely, Latinos represented a smaller share of prison releases than either Whites or African Americans (26% Latinos, 40.5% African Americans, and 32.2% Whites). NCLR points out, "the Latino data are troubling because they suggest that, if these proportions hold constant.... the share of the overall prison population that is Latino may grow."

The P.P.E.C members just like most other churches (whether they are Adventist or not) are commuters, and because they live so far, they are not affected with the things that plague the residents within close proximity of the church. The church has a membership of 1,491 members on the books, and on average, we have about 500 people who show up for service. Some of the individuals in that group are obviously not members, and I would say one-third of them are visitors.

As far as the congregation, P.P.E.C varies on the financial and educational scale. We have those from both the unemployed and the employed and the formally educated and the informally educated (I never like to call a person uneducated because they did not attend or graduate from a parochial school). There are members of the congregation who tout six-figure salaries, but they are not the type of members who wear their wealth on their sleeves. For most of them, the only way to know what kind of money they are making would be to follow them outside of the church to see what vehicle they are driving, and even that is not a determining factor. There are lawyers, judges, and health physicians who make significant contributions to the church. There are also members who have their own businesses and are doing quite well in the community. On the other hand, we have members who are struggling to make ends meet. Some of them are struggling to maintain and even pay their children's tuition. As some of these parents make a valiant effort to send their children to the Adventist school, they cannot keep up with the demand to pay tuition. The body of elders comprises individuals who range from the bottom of the so- called social ladder to the top.

It is quite embarrassing that what we read, and the word preached from the Scriptures, encourages us to do more work outside of the church than inside. Because of this persistent disconnect and lethargic attitude towards the "least of these," the P.P.E.C has become just another building on a street that takes up parking once a week, which is not a unique situation to most churches. In the East Oak Cliff area of Dallas, there are eighteen churches. Out of the eighteen churches in that area, thirteen of them are of the Baptist faith including the famous Good Street Baptist Church. The P.P.E.C is the only Seventh-day Adventist church. Although we are outnumbered, like most other Adventist churches, we believe that doing the work for political activism and social justice is for other denominations. Our denomination/church should focus on issues concerning eschatology and religious freedom. This is ludicrous, according to a percept study done in 2010 on the zip code where the church resides, as a plethora of issues were discovered. The study provided information in regards to faith beliefs, greatest needs, community issues, and worship styles. Some of the issues that were very important to subjects were neighborhood gangs, neighborhood crime and safety, racial/ethnic prejudice, and affordable housing. The stress level of the residents appeared to be critically high because these community problems were resulting in their health deteriorating. The primary concern of 40-43% of households said that maintaining health was a primary concern for them.

Examples of these stressors are households below the poverty line, adults with a high school diploma, households with a single mother, and basic necessities such as food, housing, and employment opportunities. According to the study, it was also discovered that 1827% of the residents were concerned about finding employment opportunities. The national average is 14%.

Only 55.9% of the population over the age of twenty-five has graduated from high school, which is extremely low in comparison to the national average of 80.4%. All of these are factors that contribute to crime, which increases the prison population. The P.P.E.C has had this information in their possession for years, but they have done very little to address the issues.

Not only is the African-American population in this area aging, but the demographics are changing rapidly as well. According to the percept study, the rate of Hispanics and Latinos moving into the East Oak Cliff area is growing rapidly. The statistics show that 83-99% of the residents within a five-mile radius of the church is Hispanic and Latino. The burst of population for this group was astronomical. In comparison to blacks they have doubled and in some cases tripled in numbers.

The Southern sector of the Dallas area is infested with unhealthy options for the citizens, which should not be used as an excuse because we can do better. The unhealthy options are creating premature deaths that are linked to an unstable mindset and diet. Most of these foods tastes great, but are doused in monosodium glutamate (MSG), which masks the real flavor of the food. According to the website "foodispower.org:"

Studies have found that wealthy districts have three times as many supermarkets as poor ones do, that white neighborhoods contain an average of four times as many supermarkets as predominantly black ones do, and that grocery stores in African-American communities are usually smaller with less selection. People's choices about what to eat are severely limited by the options available to them and what they can afford—and many food deserts contain an overabundance of fast food chains selling cheap "meat" and dairy-based foods that are high in fat, sugar and salt.

Bob Sunburn says that, "Our state has the largest 'grocery gap' in the nation, which means it has a lower number of supermarkets per capita than any other state. This shortage of supermarkets creates very real barriers to the access of healthy foods, particularly for lower-income Texans." When you drive in areas like Pleasant Grove, South Dallas, West Dallas, you are bombarded with liquor store after liquor store, Chinese food restaurants, and mom-and-pop fried chicken shacks. In order to find healthier choices, you would have to drive to some of the more affluent areas in Dallas. Coupled with the lack of access to healthy options, there are a plethora of payday loan advance shops, pawn shops, and title loan advance businesses. Everything that is out there to hurt, exploit, and eviscerate the poor is available to them.

One of the major needs of the P.P.E.C is an increased sensitivity to those that are marginalized. The church has no means by which we challenge systems and organizations that blatantly seek to keep the poor and the rich in their current status or bracket group. We do a great job at feeding, clothing, and ministering, but we are completely oblivious to what is happening in our society. We are also very insular, which makes us very much out of touch as well. Most of the programs and events that are developed are predominately attended by other Seventh-day Adventists. We market and promote these events to other Adventist churches. Most residents who live within proximity of the church do not know who we are, most likely. They are aware of the fact that we show up every week in very nice vehicles and consume the neighborhood parking. This kind of behavior has to stop. Not only are we irrelevant to the community, but we are also irrelevant to local organizations, ministers and leaders.

THE OPERATING SYSTEM

2

Darren Wilson is the officer that was charged in the shooting death of the unarmed young man Michael Brown. Local leaders and ministers of the Oak Cliff area have been meeting to discuss a plan of action for the future; unfortunately, Adventist ministers have not been invited to the table. The non-invitation is a reflection of the reputation that the ministers and leaders within the Adventist community possess. It is clearly known by others that Adventists do not want anything to do with the fight against injustice. Our answers to the ills of society are to pray and to wait, or "All things work together for good to those that love the Lord and to those who are called according to His purpose." If that is the case, then blacks would still have to deal with Jim Crow segregation.

It is understood that congregations are simply a reflection of their pastors. Therefore, I cannot hold them accountable, for they are only doing what is projected to them. Through my spiritual autobiography I realized that my education has a lot to do with a church's total disregard for issues of social justice and political activism. There was nothing black about my education. I never read the works of Frederick Douglass, W.E.B. Dubois, and Howard Thurman. The educational experience was one-sided and expressed the thoughts of an imperialistic view of the Scriptures. The education received could be viewed as a "top down theology." That is a theology that does not see yourself in the text. You do not see yourself as blind Bartimaeus, but only as those who are telling him to be quiet. Therefore, if you are not Bartimaeus, then you will never be able to ask the questions that the text is calling for. Why is Bartimaeus blind, poor, and begging by the roadside? Are others in society blind, poor, and begging by the roadside? Can it be that today there are those that are blind, poor and begging by the roadside because of unjust policies and mandates that target those that do not have a seat at the table? Most Adventist ministers do not interrogate the text, myself included. Instead, we would look at blind Bartimaeus simply as an individual who wants forgiveness from Jesus. We will not even take the time to understand the context of the text and realize that he is in Jericho, the same city that Jesus used as a setting to tell the story of the man that was beaten and robbed by the roadside.

The problem with our theology is that 95% of Adventist ministers share the same views and thought processes when it comes to interpreting the Scriptures. We lack that social justice bone in our bodies, and if that is not there then we cannot expect our churches to be any different. Adventist ministers go through the same system, and we all receive the same education. The only thing that differs is the name of the school on the degree. Nine times out of ten you will not be employed in Adventist church structure unless you go through their system, which, in turn, means that you must think the way the system wants you to in order to operate and function within those parameters. In other words, you can only be a star and not a moon. Standing out from the crowd is not well received within the Adventist community. In the event that you stand out or become an outlier, the leadership is not prepared to handle those who think outside of the box. You must match and mirror the others, but do not try to be different. The reality is troubling because the Scriptures inform us that Jesus did not care about the status quo, but He did what He was led to do by God. Regardless of the treatment that He received, He was a rabble rouser. His intentions were not to cause problems, but He understood the relevance to agitate "things" in order to bring change. Obey Hendricks stated in his masterful work The Politics of Jesus that a person is not qualified to be a leader if he is not willing to take a few shots for the team.

This type of education is not only unique to American Adventists, but it is a worldwide pandemic. Many world church organizations have a large number of African Americans (Some would argue that blacks are the majority), and yet they have not made a formal statement about recent deaths of any of the unarmed young black men that have been murdered, or a public statement about Donald Trump's blatant disrespect and disregard to minorities and the Muslim community. This fact is troubling! There are a lot of people hurting, and there is unrest amongst parishioners. Parishioners want to know that the organization cares about the ills of society and is willing to acknowledge them on a grand scale. Even if there is no plan to combat a problem, do not ignore it and sweep it under the rug.

As a result of the spiritual journey and the context, there are clear parallels. The desire to help and assist people is deeply grounded within me. The God-given tools were implanted to help pull my brothers and sisters out of some of the holes or challenges that they find themselves in. These challenges are not selfinflicted, but they have been dug by others as traps to ensnare a certain group of people. The community and schools that nurtured me were fairly decent, but that does not mean they were adequate. The assumption was made that all high schools had paint chips falling from the ceiling, over-crowded classes, and textbooks that were ripped and old. The funding received by my school was based on the property tax, and if low income residents occupied the homes surrounding the schools, then that school was viewed as a 'dropout factory.' A prison pipeline was created to put more dollars in the pockets of those that have investments and stocks in the prison industry. On the other side of the town, there is a school that receives the best teachers, books, and offers the best education that the

United States of America can give a student. Their schools become pipelines to ivy-league schools and opportunities of which black and brown children are challenged to receive an acceptance letter.

In retrospect, when looking at the training received in my adolescent to late teen years in comparison with my theological training, there is a tremendous deficit. The deficit exists because during the teenage years, I received an education that believed in social promotion. In public school most mornings, the teacher would hand out a paper and tell us to fill it out. Communication was rare, and the inspiration to do more was not fostered by most teachers. There were some teachers that tried to do all that they could to inspire us to take our education seriously. At that time, there was not anything more compelling than watching boys dress to impress the girls and seeing the attention they garnered from wearing the latest fashions. There was no true African presence in my curriculum, but only a distorted view of American history. The only vivid memory of American history is that we were slaves, and then we were freed to help fight in the Civil War. School was simply: you were expected to learn facts so that you can pass a test.

The consciousness and self-awareness that I needed was not instilled in me at the academic level. Most of the time, a young black boy is not going to research and look deeper into his ancestry and history. He will take what is given to him, believe it, and in some cases argue with anyone who tries to disagree with it. My foundation was weak while being bombarded with negative pictures of African-American men in the media; I was at a crossroads.

The worst educational experience was that of my theological training. It is considered the worst because thousands of dollars were paid to obtain it. Parts of the theological training were beneficial and helped me to develop personally, but the training received was not relevant to the immediate context. Unaware and oblivious to the needs of the disenfranchised, I began to embrace the oppressor and hate the oppressed. Statements like "social justice has no place in the Scriptures" or "Those matters don't need to be discussed from the pulpit," were regular comments that were made during my matriculation. Statements like "ministers should never get involved in the political arena because God has no place there" were deeply rooted within. It was not until my seminary experience that some of my friends introduced me to the sermons of Freddie Haynes III, Jeremiah Wright, Charles G. Adams, and Otis Moss.

As an associate pastor in Harlem, NY, my opinion began to change. Systemic racism and the unfair treatment of the poor became clear to me. It was at that point that I realized a change needed to occur, and it needed to start from within. There was a need to retool, reequip, and reeducate. Upon moving to Dallas, I saw poverty at a whole new level. There definitely is a difference between the two worlds, south of the Mason-Dixon line. In my opinion, New York has undercover racism; but in Texas, the racism is overt and "in your face." As I walk down the streets of Dallas, Houston, and San Antonio and see the torn up neighborhoods, I see brand new, state-of-the-art pawnshops, payday loan advance shops, and title loan shops, and I ask myself, "How can this be?" I have noticed, on average, two or three liquor stores within a 500-yard radius in one area. There are supermarkets in walking distance where you cannot get healthy options. If you need to get to a Whole Foods Market in New York, you can take the bus or train because of the extensive bus and train systems. Here in Dallas, it is much more difficult, and I am sure that if some were to take public transit, they would know upon arrival that they would not be welcomed there.

My operating system was out of whack. I can remember one day I was having some difficulties with my laptop. To my discovery I was sitting next to someone who had the same laptop as I did. It was the same color, same specs, and same design; there was nothing off about it. I noticed that his computer was moving faster than mine; it had features that I did not possess on my laptop. My computer, on the other hand, kept freezing; it was moving slower than it normally did, and it just felt really old. It took the computer about five minutes to complete a simple task. Eventually, I swallowed my pride and asked my neighbor about his laptop. Why is it, that your laptop seems to be moving quicker and looks a lot better than mine? His response to me was that my r computer was moving so slow, because I had not updated my operating system. He said, "You can have all these features, but you need to update your operating system."

As I thought about that day, I realized something: my operating system was out of date. I was operating on a system within my mainframe that did not speak to the issues concerning my people and neighborhood. Although I looked like other ministers, the operating system that I was working with prevented me from preaching and doing what is required of me.

I had to do something about this. My teachings, learning, and understanding needed to be updated. I was desirous of a broader perspective in regards to biblical social justice and activism. I wanted to unlearn imperialistic theology and replace it with restorative theology. In an attempt to find, to resolve and to provide assistance through prayer and consultation, the Lord guided me to United Theological Seminary, where I saw the Gardner C. Taylor Scholars cohort's social justice and political activism. Since the church is a reflection of the pastor, if I wanted to witness change, then the mandate begins with me, and I needed to be the champion that led the way to change. For an Adventist to be successful in doing social justice work in the community that minister must be willing to reach across whatever obstacles and engage with others in various denominations. Starting a social justice ministry is foreign to most of us, and the framework to establish such a program is grounded in the doctoral work of the existing cohort.

If the Adventist minister plans to be relevant in the community then he or she must have a plan to gain a greater understanding by interpreting the Scriptures from a social justice point of view. In order to establish a social justice ministry, it will require work. The minister must carry a burden not only for the members but for the community as well. As clergy men and women, we cannot continue to stand and preach without a social justice tone from the pulpits that we use. There is a call for change. There is a need to speak truth to power inside of the church and outside of the church. We cannot be afraid to put the spotlight on discrimination and the marginalization of female counterparts in ministry.

WHAT HELPED ME

3

I am always intrigued and mesmerized by speakers who can marry contemporary issues of injustice with the sacred text. In listening to others bringing the issues that plague us as humans on race relations and racism to the pulpit in light of the text, I am amazed. I am left to wonder how in the world did they see that? From where did they get that thought in the text? It is clear that their training was totally opposite from the one that I obtained. As silly as this may sound, I wanted to learn how to study the Bible with a prophetic lens and a voice that speaks truth to power. Through learning and studying with cohort partners, I was praying for balance in my thinking and comprehension of the Scriptures. This appears to be the missing link in my studies, and United Theological Seminary will assist in bridging the gap. Accomplishing the goal will be my primary responsibility, and various disciplines must be instituted such as being self-taught and self-read, but the guidance will be helpful in my matriculation.

TRUST THE PROCESS

You and I are going to go through a process of reeducation and retraining until we provide a solid foundation to build upon. Having a clear canvas to work upon will help us to develop a plan of action for my congregation. The grounds of the study will trace the roots of the Eurocentric theology in the Adventist church. Furthermore, it will propose an indictment on Adventist theology that has no interest in the black presence and/ or the down-trodden. It is important for the reader to know and understand the origins of imperialistic theology. The section of the project on imperialistic theology will be helpful to other ministers, not just blacks, but anyone who is interested in the topic of social justice. In doing so, it will create a place of vulnerability and provide a first-hand account of what has been extended to me.

As you join me on this journey by the end of this book, the completed work will give greater insight with regards to why churches operate and function within the realms of the exclusion of social justice. Therefore, that segment of the research must be comprehensive for you the reader to grasp the understanding and relevance. The Lord is calling you to speak truth to power and the completed work will be "decent and in order," without slander or defaming the historical educational experience. It is no coincidence that my spiritual journey has led you and me to have a passion for justice.

NEXT STEPS

4

When the process is complete, my prayer is that you will be equipped to give the body of Christ something to grasp and continue even in your absence. This statement is made because in the Adventist system most pastors average about four years with a particular congregation. Perhaps, you are leader in a different faith and are having difficulty with leading your congregation to understand the need for social justice; then this journey will be beneficial to you as well. In short, we are passing through to do a particular job; that is why it is extremely important that whatever is done, it is done to leave a legacy that others can benefit from. It is my belief that it is our job to make a church better for the next pastor that will obtain it. In the event that you are called to pastor another church in an obscure district, the legacy will continue despite your absence. The desire is to inspire the laity to continue to be abreast and aware of various things that are plaguing the voiceless. The project will spark awareness in the local context to ensure and establish meaningful dialogue with local community affairs.

I am also praying that this book can be beneficial to other ministers and not just ministers in the Adventist denomination. Many protestant churches have thrown in the white flag and are willing to accept things as they are. Then there are other ministers who have tried to change things, but, because of resistance, they too have raised the white flag of surrender. This book is written to inspire and make lives of other ministers a bit easier when they are ready to tackle injustice.

One of the things that I dislike about myself and about other faith denominations, is that when there is a crisis, that is when we wake up. This book was written while our nation was and is witnessing a tremendous increase of police brutality on black and brown citizens. The most recent case being the nonindictment of Officer Darren Wilson; there is this black consciousness that has arisen. The assault is on immigrants being housed and imprisoned in detention centers. The unfortunate truth is that black consciousness rises but dies after several months have passed. As a community we cannot afford to just have emotional responses to injustice, because that will not get us anywhere. Every day there are crimes against the voiceless that go under the radar, and we need a group that has been empowered to lend a voice to the voiceless.

The Lord has provided the burden of social justice that can be used as a vehicle to help educate young theology majors and bible scholars alike. If all goes well the book will open up a discussion about the development of a social justice curriculum for theology majors. As of now-- I could be wrong I don't know of any curriculum in our schools that can teach and prepare young pastors to make an impact in churches that are in impoverished communities. The curriculum will definitely teach them to see social justice and political issues within the text and introduce them to some of the black scholars who have done some of the most prolific work in that area.

In summation, I want this process that the Lord is taking us through to make us better people for His service, and not simply to make a better pastor, better fathers, uncles, and brothers as well. I have two beautiful daughters, and I am aware that they will grow up in a world that will shamefully judge them by the color of their skin. It is our responsibility to teach those that follow us how to navigate in a world that expects nothing much from them. My wife and daughters are the first and primary flock that God has given to me to protect. I know that my development as a man, a father, and a minister will be beneficial to them. My favorite preacher Dr. Frederick D. Haynes III tells a story about the moment he went to a convention to do a presentation. When he walked through the door, he noticed that someone left a wedge there to hold the door open. The person who left the wedge in the door was courteous enough to say that just because I got through this door, I'm going to leave it open so that somebody else can get through this door as well. That's so important for all of us to learn. When we get through doors, it's only right that we leave a wedge so that others can get through the door as well.

BIBLICAL FOUNDATIONS

5

It is clear that there is some sense of indifference or lack of interest that resides within the church as it relates to the necessities within the community. The existence of apathy is a direct result of limited biblical education, and the disconnection exists because of the inability to connect. For many years the theology of charity has been a sufficient outreach to the community. However, a theology of charity is not enough; we need a theology of public policy. A theology of charity will result in a cyclical pattern that finds us doing the same thing over and over. Charity must lead to justice. Biblical public policy seeks ways to encourage and help individuals stand on their own two feet so that they can open doors for others.

Many congregations are commuter churches with the majority of the membership living outside of the neighborhood, and they are not touched with the issues of the people. Membership gives the appearance of trafficking into the community once a week for a few hours, and then migrating back to their communities for the next six days. In that one day the only effort to engage the neighbors is done by a group of maybe ten to fifteen people of the congregation that seats approximately five hundred people.

It is apparent that congregations adopt the personality of leadership and are a reflection of their pastors. Therefore, if ministers are trained at institutions that promote Eurocentric interpretations of the Scriptures, it is almost impossible to use the very same texts to speak truth to power. In most instances higher education institutions and seminaries have become factories that pump out ministers who are divorced from their African heritage in the Word of God. They also become ministers who cannot preach a prophetic word that champions the rights of the marginalized and tears down systems of oppression that exists from within and outside. The goal is to create awareness to the local congregation that will expand beyond the four walls to a larger scale. In an attempt to educate the masses, which will lead to implementation, the Bible will be used to provide the educational framework. Both Old and

New Testament scriptures will be researched. The Old Testament scripture is Nehemiah 2:1-5 and the New Testament scripture is Luke 4:16-18. Both testaments provide a comprehensive spotlight on the importance and impact of the necessity to develop outreach programs that will aid the community.

Nehemiah 2:1-5 states,

"In the month of Nisan, in the twentieth year of King Artaxerxes, when wine was served him, I carried the wine and gave it to the king. Now, I had never been sad in his presence before. So the king said to me, "Why is your face sad, since you are not sick? This can only be sadness of the heart." Then I was very much afraid. I said to the king, "May the king live forever! Why should my face not be sad, when the city, the place of my ancestors' graves, lies waste, and its gates have been destroyed by fire?" Then the king said to me, "What do you request?" So I prayed to the God of heaven. Then I said to the king, "If it pleases the king, and if your servant has found favor with you, I ask that you send me to Judah, to the city of my ancestors' graves, so that I may rebuild it."

The Old Testament text is used because of Nehemiah's concern for his brothers and sisters back in Jerusalem. He is in the king's palace working as a cupbearer, but yet the news of the destruction of the walls has propelled him to go help those in need. The exegesis of this text will draw attention to several things including: the fact that Nehemiah is connected to his history; he is concerned about the destruction; he is willing to depart his current location to assist in building up the community, and he develops an infrastructure for the Israelites to inhabit.

The selected New Testament text is Luke's account of Jesus in the temple reading from the book of Isaiah in Luke 4:16-18.

So He came to Nazareth, where He had been brought up. And as His custom was, He went into the synagogue on the Sabbath day, and stood up to read. And He was handed the book of the prophet Isaiah. And when He had opened the book, He found the place where it was written: "The Spirit of the Lord is upon Me, Because He has anointed Me To preach the gospel to the poor; He has sent Me to heal the brokenhearted, To proclaim liberty to the captives And recovery of sight to the blind, To set at liberty those who are oppressed; To proclaim the acceptable year of the Lord."

In this passage Jesus returns to the place of His birth and chooses to read a passage from Isaiah 61:1, 2 and Isaiah 58:6. His message is powerful because He describes that His ministry on earth is to preach the gospel to the poor, to heal the broken hearted, to preach deliverance to the captives and recovering sight to the blind, to set at liberty those that have been bruised, and to proclaim the acceptable year of the Lord.

One can see that from both passages, the individuals in the periscope are addressing legitimate needs in the community. The purpose of this chapter is to draw attention to the fact that there is a biblical mandate to share with those who are less fortunate. The Bible admonishes us that we ought to seek to serve others with the gifts that we have. Our capitalistic society has infected us with this insatiable hunger to serve ourselves and to cultivate and capture as many material things that we can in order to make the world a better place for ourselves. Our mission has been forgotten, and our focus has become blurred. We have been caught up in the web of a false doctrine that has been spewed from the pulpits, that encourages us to "name it and claim it," "reach out and grab it," "pull it down," and "it's your season" instead of a consciousness to acknowledge the least of these that are amongst us. We have in some sense done a great disservice to our listeners when we only give them sermons to shout about, not enough to think about.

The next chapter is a careful step-by-step process to interpret the text in its original setting, with specific attention to key words in each passage. After both texts are examined, a context will be bridged from the historical biblical setting to the contemporary society.

THE PLACE OF MY ANCESTORS' GRAVES

6

Nehemiah 2:1-5 states,

"In the month of Nisan, in the twentieth year of King Artaxerxes, when wine was served him, I carried the wine and gave it to the king. Now, I had never been sad in his presence before. So the king said to me, "Why is your face sad, since you are not sick? This can only be sadness of the heart." Then I was very much afraid. I said to the king, "May the king live forever! Why should my face not be sad, when the city, the place of my ancestors' graves, lies waste, and its gates have been destroyed by fire?" Then the king said to me, "What do you request?" So I prayed to the God of heaven. Then I said to the king, "If it pleases the king, and if your servant has found favor with you, I ask that you send me to Judah, to the city of my ancestors' graves, so that I may rebuild it."

The Book of Nehemiah is named after the author. Scholars suggest that the books of

Nehemiah and Ezra are to be read together. According to Jewish tradition, the books are treated as one volume. It is impossible to understand the context of Nehemiah without doing some investigation in the Book of Ezra. Although Nehemiah is not mentioned in the Book of Ezra we do see, Ezra's name mentioned numerous times in the Book of Nehemiah. In order to be true to the text, it is important that we do not confuse the "Nehemiah" mentioned in Ezra 2:2 as the "Nehemiah son of Halchaliah," who is the subject of this Old Testament reflection.

The major themes are consistent in the Book of Ezra and Nehemiah. Ezra was a priest that focused on the renewal of Israel's spirituality and the law of God. He was also very instrumental in the rebuilding of the temple as well as the purification of the children of Israel by prompting them to put away their pagan wives. Historians have shown that the children of Israel had acquired many of the customs and traditions of the Babylonians while they were in captivity. Ezra's job was to restore exclusivity and purity amongst the Israelites, by turning them back to the law of the Lord. Nehemiah's primary concern was rebuilding the walls. According to the Andrews University Study Bible, "Social action is another important theological topic in Nehemiah. Nehemiah 5 reminds us that social justice cannot be separated from religious reforms." In the account written about Nehemiah it is discovered that the work of rebuilding the walls could not have been done without the help of those that were in the community.

There is little information about Nehemiah. All we know is that his name means "the Lord Comforted" and he is the son of Hacaliah. The reason for the identification is so that readers would not confuse him with the others named Nehemiah. Some scholars suggest that Nehemiah came from a royal background, which is why he had the job of the cupbearer. This notion was disputed because there is no evidence to prove it. However, it has been proven that Nehemiah was a descendant from the tribe of Judah. Another speculation is that Esther recommended Nehemiah for the position.

The story of Nehemiah opens up in chapter 1:1, "And it came to pass in the month of Chisleu, in the twentieth year as I was in Shushan the palace." The chapter informs us that while he was in the palace, his brother Hananias well as some other men came to visit him. Hanani was not his biological brother, but it was a term that was loosely used by other Orientals. However, it is believed that Hanani was part of his family. Upon seeing them Nehemiah proceeds to ask them questions. How are the conditions among the Jews who had escaped captivity and Jerusalem? The news that Nehemiah heard struck a chord in his heart. Nehemiah 1:3 says, "They said to me, 'Things are not going well for those who returned to the province of Judah. They are in great trouble and disgrace. The wall of Jerusalem has been torn down, and the gates have been destroyed by fire.'" In the next verse, the scripture indicates that after hearing this news Nehemiah sat down and wept. In fact, for days he spent time morning, fasting, and praying to the God of Heaven.

Nehemiah works for King Artaxerxes I. He is the third son of Xerxes and Amestris, ruler of the Persian from 464-424 BC. The Faith Study Bible refers to Artaxerxes as such:

The "most remarkable" of all the kings of Persia for a "gentle and noble spirit" (Art. 1.1).

"Artaxerxes" is the Greek form of the Old Persian artakhsassa, meaning "having a kingdom of justice." "Artaxerxes" was likely a throne name; Josephus records that Artaxerxes I's name before his accession was Cyrus (Ant. 11.6). According to Plutarch, Artaxerxes I was nicknamed "long-armed" (Greek markocheir; Latin longimanus) because his right arm was longer than his left (Art. 1.1). There were two other Persian kings identified by this name: Artaxerxes II (404–358 BC), and Artaxerxes III (359–338 BC).

King Artaxerxes received the moniker as "gentle and noble" for his kindness that he showed towards Ezra and Nehemiah although some theologians would argue that his willingness to do this was more providential to him than to the Jews. King Artaxerxes felt that it would be better to be an ally than an enemy to the Israelites.

It is in this chapter particularly in verse eighteen that we discover Nehemiah's job title. He is known as the cupbearer to the King. According to the Expositors commentary,

The office held by Nehemiah was not one of political rank. He was a palace slave, not a minister of state like Joseph or Daniel. But among the household servants he would take a high position. The cupbearer shad a special privilege of admission to the august presence of their sovereign in his most private seclusion.

Nehemiah was not a politician, but he knew that he had influence. The cupbearers were entrusted to protect the king. The cupbearer r had to be trusted because enemies of wealth would attempt to bribe them so that they could poison the king. The duty of the cupbearer was to taste the wine before it was given to the king. Therefore, the life of the king was invested in the hands of the cupbearer. Only a select few were chosen to be a cupbearer. Obviously, he was a trusted and good worker for King Artaxerxes. It is safe to believe that he was ranked highest among all other cupbearers in the palace. The Expositors Commentary elaborates more on this idea,

Thus, the cupbearers would become "favourites." At all events, it is plain that Nehemiah was regarded with peculiar favour by the king he served. No doubt he was a faithful servant, and his fidelity in his position of trust at court was a guarantee of similar fidelity in a more responsible and far more trying office.

Nehemiah was distraught by the news of what happened to his kinsmen in Jerusalem. As we can see from the text, that, although Nehemiah was not in Jerusalem, there is a legitimate concern for the destroyed walls. The second chapter of Nehemiah, verses one through five, provides an interpretation in regards to Nehemiah's desire to leave the palace for pandemonium.

Chapter two moves from the prayer to God to the request of King Artaxerxes. Verse one says, "And it came to pass in the month of Nisan...." In the previous chapter Nehemiah receives the news from Hanani and the brethren in the month of Chislev. According to the Hebrew calendar the month of Chislev would reflect the later quarter of a calendar year, possibly November or December. The month of Nisan would have been March or April. Clearly the time period that Nehemiah got the news and when he decided to approach King Artaxerxes was a span of approximately four months. The time of the year is relevant because the month of Nisan as the beginning of the Hebrew calendar sparked the idea of new beginnings and a fresh start. According to the Harper's Bible Dictionary,

Nisan, the first month of the OT year. Nisan is an Akkadian loan word and forms part of the Babylonian system of lunar month names taken over by the Jews some time after the Exile. Nisan falls in the spring (March-April) and corresponds to the earlier Hebrew designation. The festival of Passover is celebrated in mid-Nisan, and it also marks the time of Jesus' crucifixion.

Nehemiah seizes this moment as a reminder of God's delivering hand on behalf of the Israelites that were in bondage by the Babylonians. When God removed them from the hard labor, he established His covenant with Israel as a Protector and a God that will never abandon them. The month of Nisan for any Israelite will be a reminder of what was and to look forward for great things to come.

Although Nisan is a time of renewals and reminders of deliverance and freedom, Nehemiah is still extremely distraught by the news concerning those in Jerusalem. The rest of the verse says that it is in the twentieth year of King Artaxerxes Longimanus. This is the same king that appears in the Book of Ezra 7:1. The second half of the verse informs us that Nehemiah had took the wine in the presence of the king and gave it to him, and then proceeds to say, "Now I had never been sad in his presence before." The Hebrew word for 'sad' is 'רַע (r(ע), it can also mean troubled, miserable, or distressed. J. Swanson states that this sadness is, "pertaining to an attitude or emotion of anxiety and worry." It is the same grief that is expressed in Psalm 94:13, "That You may give him rest from the days of adversity, until the pit is dug for the wicked." This Psalm is refuge for the righteous. The verse points to the fact that there is no repose for those that have been attacked by their enemies whether physically or mentally. Nehemiah finds himself without rest because the weight he carries deep down inside. However, the concerns that Nehemiah carries for his people is now evident and is expressed within his facial emotions.

The countenance of Nehemiah proposed a grave risk for the cupbearer. It is known that a cupbearer could face execution if he were to appear before the king with a look of displeasure. Esther 4:2 says, "He went as far as the front of the king's gate, for no one might enter the kings' gate clothed with sackcloth." Kings were protected from those that were mourning. Through the text we see that

Nehemiah's distress was visibly apparent when he appeared before King Artaxerxes. It is suggested that the sadness that Nehemiah possessed extends beyond the destruction of the walls but also the cause of the destruction.

Nehemiah served in the palace c. 444 B.C. Therefore, it is safe to believe that the news of the destruction of walls in Jerusalem occurred around this time. We should not confuse the destruction of the walls with the havoc wreaked by Nebuchadnezzar in 587 B.C. The timelines donot agree with each other. The context of the destruction has to be read within the context of Ezra 4:7-23. Those verses record a correspondence that was written to King Artaxerxes. In the letter local leadership of the Persian administration informed the king that the rebuilding of the wall was rooted in rebellion and dissension. Ezra 4:12-13 states,

Let it be known to the king that the Jews who came up from you have come to us at Jerusalem, and are building the rebellious and evil city, and are finishing its walls and repairing the foundations. Let it now be known to the king that, if this city is built and the walls completed, they will not pay tax, tribute, or custom, and the king's treasury will be diminished.

Immediately the king responds with a decree in verse twenty-one to make these men cease from building the walls until a command is given by King Artaxerxes. Upon receiving the correspondence, we are told that the Persians went up in haste to Jerusalem adjacent to the Jews and by force of arms made them cease. The sadness and suffering that caught Nehemiah off guard arethe mere fact that the cessation of work and the destruction of the walls were sanctioned by the very king that he is a cupbearer for.

One of the results of that siege was the very existence of Nehemiah's Jewish colony in Babylon. Rather, we must look to the events resulting from the correspondence in Ezra 4 :7– 23 and dated in the reign of Artaxerxes I. The destruction reported to Nehemiah must have taken place sometime after Ezra's mission in the seventh year of that reign and before the delegation headed by Hanani came to Susa. This reconstruction would fully account for Nehemiah's surprise and distress in that he would immediately realize that his Persian master was responsible for the condition of Jerusalem and its inhabitants.

It must have been difficult for Nehemiah to request of the king to send him to rebuild the very thing that he was instrumental in destroying. It must have been difficult for Nehemiah to hold these emotions in as he tries to perform his daily chores with a heavy heart. According to the New King James Version of verse two, the text says that the king notices Nehemiah's sadness and proceeds to ask him, "Why is your face sad, since you are not sick? This is nothing but sorrow of the heart. So I became dreadfully afraid." The New King James Version was the only translation that used the word "dreadfully" to describe Nehemiah's fear in the presence of King Artaxerxes. The English Standard Version, New Revised Standard Version, and New International Version all say, "I was very much afraid."

Only the more contemporary version like the Message Bible uses the word 'agitated' instead of 'dreadful' or 'very much.' According to the Hebrew Bible the word used is יָרֵא (yā·rē(')), which means, "be frightened, i.e., be in a state of feeling great distress, and deep concern of pain or unfavorable circumstance." Strong's Concordance also uses the synonym "dreadful" to describe the feeling that Nehemiah had in the presence of the king. The word 'agitated' gives the connotation that Nehemiah became angry, annoyed, upset, or perturbed, which has limited validity because a display of outward act or emotion before the king could have resulted in execution for Nehemiah. The definition of the word can also suggest that the fear represented in verse two is in relation to a respect and awe that Nehemiah has for the king.

It was the visible presence of the sadness in Nehemiah that prompts this impromptu dialogue between King Artaxerxes and Nehemiah. In this discussion the word sad or sadness is mentioned four times in the dialogue. The king uses the word "sorrow" or, עֹר (rōᵃʿ), which is only an alternative to the aforementioned רַע (răʿ). It is the trouble and distress that motivates him to make his request known to the king. Amazingly, the dialogue begins with King Artaxerxes asking Nehemiah, "Why is your face sad, since you are not sick? This is nothing but sorrow of heart?" The conversation engages in a series of questions, and answers. As each question is asked, Nehemiah expresses his displeasure.

Artaxerxes is depicted as interested and concerned about his court favorite, direct and probing in his questioning, and pleased to grant every request. Nehemiah externally displays proper respect and attention to court etiquette in his responses to the king. But as the structure of the passage makes clear, we can observe an internal growth in confidence as Nehemiah becomes increasingly assured that God has answered his four-month period of prayer affirmatively.

Nehemiah's exchange with the king reminds us that his confidence is given because of an unseen character who is instrumental in making sure that all the provisions are supplied so that the work can move forward.

In Nehemiah's exchange with King Artaxerxes, he tells him the reason for his sadness. His words are, "Why should not my face not be sad, when the city, the place of my fathers' tombs, lies waste, and its gates are burned with fire." Nehemiah chooses to use 'city' instead of 'Jerusalem,' scholars suggest that this is because he does not want to disclose the location that he wants to rebuild. Nehemiah is passionate when he says "the place of my fathers' tombs, lies waste."   A more contemporary translation of the text would be, 'the place where my ancestors graves, are destroyed.' James E. Smith says,

Nehemiah made no effort to evade the king's question. He told Artaxerxes that his sadness was justifiable in view of the desolate condition of Jerusalem, "the place of my fathers' tombs." The reference to the tomb was a stroke of genius. Persians were paranoid about respect for the dead and proper burial. The phrase evoked immediate sympathy from this monarch who only a few years before had ordered the work of rebuilding Jerusalem to cease.

It's absolutely clear that Nehemiah is not your average cupbearer; being in the temple of the Persians has given Nehemiah insight into the customs and traditions of the Persians. To know that they regarded the burial and death of their ancestors was enough to move Artaxerxes to grant his request to restore the walls of Jerusalem.

It is also important to mention that Nehemiah has a deep connection to his ancestry. Warren Wiersbe points to this fact in his work "Be Determined." Warren writes, "Nehemiah was the kind of person who cared. He cared about the traditions of the past and the needs of the present. He cared about the hopes for the future. He cared about his heritage, his ancestral city, and the glory of his God. He revealed this caring attitude in four different ways." Nehemiah knew his history. He knew the stories, and traditions of his forefathers, which prompted the desire in him to make a difference.

It is documented that history is very important to the Jewish nation. Today Jewish children are encouraged to learn the Torah and memorize the Psalms. Education is stressed heavily amongst the Jews. Historians would point out that every time the Jews went into exile their books would be burned. In order to prevent that problem, Jews would commit thousands of literature to memory so that their tradition would never be lost. Joseph Telushkin says this about modern Jews, "They are Jewishly illiterate. The most basic terms in Judaism and the most significant facts in Jewish history and contemporary Jewish life, are either vaguely familiar or unknown to most modern Jews. They can tell you the three components of the Trinity but have an infinitely harder time explaining mitzvah." It is evident that even though Nehemiah was not seen as a religious leader like Ezra, but more as a political leader, he still was aware of his ancestry.

Nehemiah tells the king not only are the graves ruined, but also the city gates have been burned with fire. City walls are very important. Walls provide structure, safety, and protection. The walls were significant in the protection and preservation of the inhabitants. The Bible Reader's Companion elaborates on the walls, "Unwalled cities in ancient times had no defense against enemies. More significant at this time, unwalled cities were dismissed as insignificant. Thus, for Jerusalem to lack walls was a disgrace to the city God had chosen—and brought dishonor to the Lord!" Without walls Jerusalem would be susceptible to attacks from the enemy that wanted to seize their land. The Teacher Bible Commentary supports this idea as well by stating, "Cities in the ancient world were walled for protection. The walls were also symbols: Unwalled cities merited contempt. Walled cities were seen as significant. Nehemiah could not stand the thought that the city of God should not have walls, and committed himself to rebuild them." In our contemporary society walls are equally as important. Walls are used for protection, homes have fences, the White House has gates, and states have borders to keep unwanted guests out. Nehemiah could not allow himself to work in the palace while knowing that Jerusalem lied desolate.

Now that Nehemiah has stated his case, the king asks him, "What do you want?" We are informed in verse four, that before he makes his request known to the king the Revised Standard Version says that he "prays to the God of Heaven." The Hebrew word for 'prayed' is פָּלַל" palal it uses the hitpa''ēl," which gives it a reflexive stem. The reflexive stem informs that the subject acts upon himself and is not prompted by anyone or anything. It is also passive in form, which suggests that Nehemiah may have done this prayer quickly and underneath his breath. This further shows that Nehemiah would not make a move unless God was completely involved in every step of the way. Nehemiah does not pray aloud before the king because the Persians were not worshippers of the God of Heaven. In doing so would jeopardize any chance of having his requests granted. Throughout the Book of Nehemiah we are informed that he does what's called prayers of action. He prays then proceeds. In this particular verse we discover that he 'prays to the God of Heaven,' then he answers the king.

In verse five it says, "If it pleases the king, and if your servant has found favor with you, I ask that you send me to Judah, to the city of my ancestors' graves, so that I may rebuild it," as recorded in the English Standard Version. Nehemiah has confidence in knowing that since he has prayed extensively and has the strength to make the request, the king would grant the request, which is one that he would not grant to another cupbearer. Nehemiah requests to go to Jerusalem so that he could 'rebuild it,' some synonyms for the Hebrew word בָּנָה (banah) can also be, 'restore,' 'establish,' and 'develop buildings.' Each of these words is synonymous, embody and describe the work that Nehemiah wants to do. The definition for all these words provides a deeper understanding of his work. One of the definitions for the word 'restore' is to repair or renovate so as to return to its original condition. To restore the walls tells us that Nehemiah is interested in making that which was weak, new and stronger. To 'establish' the walls means to achieve permanent acceptance or recognition. Therefore, Nehemiah's job is to make sure that not only are the walls built, but that it is known by others that the walls have been erected. When someone looks to 'establish' something, it is basically conveying the idea.

Last, but definitely not least, are the words 'rebuild it.' If we were to substitute the 'rebuild it' with one of these words, we can see that Nehemiah wants to develop infrastructure for the Israelites. He is using his God given power to develop and build a city for the Israelites by empowering them to work and also giving them sustaining power to survive on their own.

WHERE HE HAD BEEN BROUGHT UP

7

For the New Testament pericope we will look at Luke 4:16-19, which is an account of Jesus reading from the Book of Isaiah. Luke is the only Gospel that records the words that Jesus read in the synagogue. Mark and Matthew tell us about Jesus reading in the temple, but we know more about his rejection, rather than the cause for the rejection. The New Revised Version records the passage as such:

So, He came to Nazareth, where He had been brought up. And as His custom was, He went into the synagogue on the Sabbath day, and stood up to read. And He was handed the book of the prophet Isaiah. And when He had opened the book, He found the place where it was written: "The Spirit of the Lord is upon Me, Because He has anointed Me To preach the gospel to the poor; He has sent Me to heal the brokenhearted, To proclaim liberty to the captives And recovery of sight to the blind, To set at liberty those who are oppressed; To proclaim the acceptable year of the Lord."

There are a many view in regards to the accuracy of the date and location that the Gospel of Luke records. Luke never identifies himself as the author of the book. According to the New International Greek Testament Commentary, "The Gospel itself is anonymous and contains no information which would enable us to identify its author, although one may draw some conclusions regarding his milieu and situation." New Testament scholars have pointed to Luke as the author of not only the third Gospel, but also to the book of Acts. Even though he doesn't identify himself throughout the texts, he does make mention of the term "we" in certain passages in the Book of Acts. Craig S. Keener uses the "we" as evidence to support the idea that Luke is the author.

Luke mentions "we" in a way peripheral to the action in passages in Acts 16 and 20-28; contrary to some scholarly constructs, "we" in historical literature almost always meant that the author was present on the occasions specified. Early tradition, attested by second-century witnesses and the early title of the book, favors Luke, traveling companion of Paul, as the author of Luke-Acts. Although the case for Luke's use of medical language has been exaggerated; the presence of educated language is consistent with the tradition of Lukan authorship.

The "educated language" of Luke is remarkable; we cannot fail to acknowledge that Luke is a purposeful and skilled writer. His classical style of Greek is important to be noted. We have already adverted to the classical style of Greek which this Evangelist writes—just what might have been expected from an educated Greek and travelled physician. But we have also observed that along with this he shows a wonderful flexibility of style, so much so, that when he comes to relate transactions wholly Jewish, where the speakers and actors and incidents are all Jewish, he writes in such Jewish Greek as one would do who had never been out of Palestine or mixed with any but Jews.

Luke has a way of communicating in that all readers of his Gospel can leave with a clear understanding of the information that he is conveying. His Gospel is said to have been written around the destruction of Jerusalem in A.D. 70. He writes to the Greek-speaking listeners in the Northern Mediterranean. His audience must have included sophisticated, affluent, and very educated people.

The purpose of the Gospel of Luke is to present the readers with an accurate description of Jesus, and the works that he displayed while on earth. Luke records instances of Jesus' life that are particular to his audience. Although is audience consists of those that are well to do, Luke is showing that Jesus is concerned with 'the least of these.' In the book True to Our Native Land, say, "Women, the lame, the hungry, and those deemed 'other, are brought to the forefront by Luke presenting Jesus as one of and for the oppressed. Lukan theology is grounded in a Jesus who comes not just to offer compassion to those who are wounded but to speak to the evil of those who wound." The Gospel of Luke is an indictment to all those who perpetuate and strengthen the power and construct the looks to keep the wheels of oppression turning. The duality of the book shows that not only was it written as a means to strengthen the early Christians' faith in Jesus, but it also served as an evangelistic effort to engage a wider audience to follow Jesus.

The gospel of Luke is to put on display the beauty and grace of Jesus. His message is directed to all those that have been marginalized and ostracized, whether it be because of economic or intrinsic social factors. The purpose of the book is summed up in Luke 19:10, "For the Son of Man came to seek out and to save the lost." He tells the children of Israel in his inaugural speech that he came to bring the gospel to the poor, heal the broken hearted, proclaim liberty to the captives, give sight to the blind, to give liberation to the oppressed, and proclaim the acceptable year of the Lord.

At Jesus' first advent, Israel had been under severe oppression from Roman rulership. Under this extreme oppression there was extreme poverty. The world in the Gospels was separated into two classes, the very rich and the very poor. Obey Hendricks alludes to this fact in The Politics of Jesus; he says, "Poverty was so widespread that the Gospel of Luke portrays Mary as giving thanks to God, that among the acts of salvation set in motion by the Messiah she carried in her womb would be filling the hungry "with good things" (Luke 1:53). To take the text in its most literal sense is to understand that the coming of the Messiah simply means that He will put an order to all things and establish fairness and equality for the needy. Howard Marshall says, "The coming of the kingdom of God should bring about a political and social revolution, bringing the ordinary life of mankind into line with the will of God."

One of the major contributing factors to the poverty in Israel was taxation. Many of the laborers in Israel were what we know as the 'working poor on top of being poor they were hit with enormous tax rates, on top of their low income. This system made sure that the rich stayed rich while the poor remained poor. High debt can also result in dislocation, hunger, and also crime. Barrabas was known as a bandit and an insurrectionist, who wanted to steal from the rich and give to the needy. It's clear that, because of such social dynamics, it would almost force people to turn to crime in order to survive.

In Israel many were renegades, insurgents, and nationalist guerrillas who rebelled against their exploitation at the hand of both the Roman provincial government and wealthy Jewish landowners; many who were priests.... Their primary goal was economic: to seize booty; and they did so, much and often. But they also had a political goal: to disrupt commerce and to discredit the ruling class by throwing the social order into disarray.

Jesus' appearance on the scene was timely as we interpret the meaning and the purpose of his work. Prior to Jesus' arrival in the Nazareth, Luke tells us about the ordeal that Jesus had while He was in the wilderness. Amazingly in the account with Jesus and Satan, we see that Satan offers Jesus power and riches. With the understanding of the economic and social dynamics of the times, Satan tries to thwart Jesus from his mission to lift the oppressed. If Jesus would have accepted the pleasures of temporal satisfaction, the action would have alleviated Jesus' credibility with the recipients of His ministry.

After the incident in the wilderness, Luke introduces another scene in the ministry of Jesus. He has now come back home of his birthplace Nazareth to minister in the synagogue. Nazareth wasn't a very large village. The village could hardly boast that it had more than five hundred residents. John 1:46 reminds us of this fact when Nathaniel boldly says, "Can anything good come from Nazareth?" This question only tells us that Nazareth was no Jerusalem or Bethlehem, but it was a small village, and not much was expected to come out of there, especially the Messiah of the world.

Guest Rabbis were often allowed to speak in local synagogues. The order of service in the local synagogue generally consisted of a private prayer upon entry into the building and the reading of the Shema. The reading of the Shema was also acknowledged as a public declaration of the Jewish faith. More prayers were offered up, and then the center of the worship was focused on the reading of the Scriptures. In most cases a passage from the Pentateuch was read, followed by more prayers. Howard Marshall says, that in the first century, "There was at least some freedom of choice of prophetic reading in the first century. Following the readings was a prayer and then came a sermon, if there was somebody competent present to give one." Luke does not give much detail in regards to how Jesus received the opportunity to read in the temple. We do not know if He was asked, or if He requested to speak on that Sabbath day. It is most certain to believe that there was some excitement to hear Jesus speak.

The scripture says in Luke 4:16, "When he came to Nazareth, where he had been brought up, he went to the synagogue on the Sabbath day, as was his custom. He stood up to read." We learn from this text that Jesus is following what he has been taught as a child. It was customary to go to the synagogue on the Sabbath day. Jews honor and respect the day of the Sabbath as the most sacred day of the week. They observe the Sabbath day as a commemoration of their deliverance from Egyptian bondage as well as a reminder of Jehovah as the Creator of the world. Visiting the synagogue on the Sabbath day was not contrary to any system that the Jews upheld. The problem is that Sabbath observance became perverted and legalistic amongst the Jews. The Sabbath is a day of God's rest from all creation. It is an invitation from God to join Him in rest. Not only was it a day to rest from labor, but it was also a time to reflect and share with neighbors. Walter Brueggemann says, "Sabbath is a practical divestment so that neighborly engagement, rather than production and consumption, defines our lives." Jesus understands the true meaning of the Sabbath. It is a day that God used for liberation of the oppressed. Isaiah 58:6, 7 says,

Is not this the fast that I choose: to lose the bonds of injustice, to undo the thongs of the yoke, to let the oppressed go free, and to break every yoke? Is it not to share your bread with the hungry, and bring the homeless poor into your house; when you see the naked, to cover them, and not to hide yourself from your own kin?

In verse thirteen God tells Isaiah to inform the Israelites not to use the Sabbath for their own personal gain or advancement. The works of Jesus always involved delivering whosoever will from bondage and establishing them with their rightful place in society. True to Our Native Land indicates,

The Sabbath must serve not only as a period of physical rest but as a time of spiritual work and worship. This worship must also include addressing the political and social needs of humankind. Jesus is the fulfillment and the completion of this holistic ideology.

The mandate is that we are invited to make the world a better place for others and simply for ourselves. The selfishness of the false Sabbath that is kept by so many has left us blind to the needs of the man lying by the roadside. Bruce Birth reminds us,

Thus, Sabbath rest is to be available to all regardless of wealth or class, and it is available to animals as well as humans (Ex. 20:10), reminding us of our common participation and worth as part of God's creation. Since we live in a world of inequalities, Sabbath then becomes a reminder that this is not as God intended it.

The same text tells us that Jesus "stood up to read," because nothing good was expected to come from Nazareth. Like most overlooked poor ghettos, it is amazing when one cracks the glass ceiling. Craig S. Keener says, "Literacy varied from one place to another in antiquity, but many estimates that on average only ten percent of the population could read and write on any significant level." He goes on to say, "More would be able to recite lines of Torah from memory than to read and understand it, but Jesus here is able to read and expound." How impactful it must have been to see Jesus, a man from their village, not only stand up read, but explain the Scriptures in such a profound way that all who listened could understand.

Jesus reads from the Book of Isaiah 61:1 whereas it says,

The spirit of the Lord God is upon me, because the Lord has anointed me; he has sent me to bring good news to the oppressed, to bind up the brokenhearted, to proclaim liberty to the captives, and release to the prisoners; to proclaim the year of the Lord's favor, and the day of vengeance of our God; to comfort all who mourn.

By Jesus reading from Isaiah he is establishing himself as a fulfillment of Old Testament, and an extension of the ministries of Elijah and Elisha. Whereas both of these men spent much of their time traveling and ministering to those that were in need.

Jesus' message is brought first of all to the people of his home town. But when Jesus goes on to speak by implication of the preaching of the gospel and the performance of mighty works among the gentiles, Nazareth begins to take on the symbolical meaning of the Jewish nation. So, the narrative takes on a more than literal significance; it becomes a paradigm not merely of the ministry of Jesus but also of the mission of the church.

Therefore, based upon the mission of the church is to bring good news to the oppressed, bind up the broken hearted, proclaim liberty to the captives, and release prisoners. "Jesus identified himself in the synagogue as God's anointed one, the Messiah, whose vocation it is to proclaim to the poor, the blind, the captives, and the oppressed the good news of the inauguration of the 'year of the Lord's favor,' when justice-in-shalom will reign."

Jesus proclaims that, "the Spirit of the Lord is upon me." The Spirit of God gives Him the liberty to fulfill the mission of bringing restoration and healing to wounded people. Listeners in the synagogue and readers of Luke's gospel would be reminded of the events that lead to this moment in the synagogue. When Jesus was baptized (Luke 3:21-22), the Holy Ghost descended on Him as an act of the Spirit of God's anointing. Now, inside of the temple before the listeners Jesus makes this public by proclaiming that the Spirit of the Lord is upon Him because the Spirit has anointed Him to do the following acts.

The anointing of the Spirit of Jesus gives credence to not only the message that is preached, but also to the work that will be done for those that fit the criteria. He is here to "preach the gospel to the poor." The New Revised Standard Version as well as other translations substitute "preach" with "proclaim." He is here to preach "the gospel." Most people would define the word 'gospel' as 'good news about Jesus.' Other definitions can be "glad tidings" or "news of victory." Mark 1:1 says, "The beginning of the gospel of Jesus Christ, the Son of God." In the book, Say to this Mountain," Mark's Story of Discipleship," we are offered an alternative definition to this word 'gospel':

Gospel was a term associated with Roman propaganda. News of a military victory on the far-flung frontiers of the Pax Romana, or of the accession to power of a new emperor, was trumpeted as "glad tidings" throughout the empire. Caesar was eulogized as a "divine man" on coins and in emperor-cults. In contrast, Mark offers decidedly non-imperial "good news" about Jesus of Nazareth, a Jewish "Christ." By using such rhetoric, Mark was engaging the struggle for hearts and minds through the popular media of the Mediterranean world.

When the gospel was preached or spoken of, there were those that were reading it in anticipation of something to come. Jesus in this text stands as one giving "news of victory" to the poor. The poor in this passage represents those that are in desperate need for deliverance from systems of oppression that were marginalizing them. Jesus gives them hope and a voice. He stands in the temple as a hero that rises up from their community and seeks to bring justice upon those that are abusing the weak. Obery Hendricks delves deeper into the idea of poverty in Israel and the Ministry of Jesus by stating:

So deep and so debilitating was the effect of impoverishment on the psycho--emotional health of his people that Jesus found it necessary to explicitly affirm their worth with the validation "Blessed are you who are poor" (Luke 6:20). And when his disciples asked him how and what to pray for, he told them to keep the poverty and hunger of the people in Israel in view y praying: 'Give us this day our daily bread' (Matthew 6:11). And to give the people hope in the face of their profound poverty, Jesus himself modeled the largesse that God's kingdom of justice promised on the occasions when he fed the thousands who had gathered to hear him share his vision of God's kingdom.

The poor in this text can also refer to those of "little value." Clearly the 'poor' in this text is no different than the poor in today's society. Since they have no money, we often deem them as having no value or as individuals who have nothing to offer. Sharon Ringe expounds on the idea of the poor in her work, Jesus, Liberation, and the Biblical Jubilee. She says:

The poor (hoi ptōchoi) are mentioned in several contexts in the Synoptic Gospels. Those contexts underline the importance of 'the poor' in Jesus' ministry and in his identity as the Christ. They also expand the meaning of the 'the poor' to include people who are socially outcast or physically disabled, as well as people who are economically disadvantaged. Among these 'poor,' then, God's saving actively is being manifested.

In Luke's Gospel Jesus is seen here as the one being a voice for the voiceless and reestablish a value system that is not based on monetary gains but simply based on the fact that they are children of God.

Jesus is sent "to preach deliverance to the captives." In modern translations Luke omits the phrase "to heal the broken hearted." Although the manuscript in Isaiah has that phrase, Luke chooses to omit it from his manuscript. It is left unknown as to why Luke chose to do so unless he felt that it was either repetitive, or there was no need for it to make his point. Hendrikson gives two possibilities:

(a)   Luke's intention was not to reproduce the entire haphtara (selection from the prophets) but only the words used by Jesus as the text for his sermon;

(b)   Correctly interpreted, the reference to "the poor" to whom the good news must be proclaimed made a further statement about "the broken-hearted" not absolutely necessary.

Based on his explanation it appears that Luke is describing the fact that, because they a poor and destitute, that leaves them broken hearted.

Jesus comes to 'preach deliverance to the captives.' Here we see the liberating element to Jesus' sermon in the synagogue. His anointing by the Spirit has giving him the authority to deliver the captives. The 'captives' in this use of the Greek can be translated as 'prisoners of war.' Jesus has come to set free those that have been conquered. The "Greek English Lexicon of the New Testament defines the captives as such:

αἰχμάλωτος: one who has been taken captive in war—'captive, prisoner of war.' ἀπέσταλκέν με κηρύξαι αἰχμαλώτοις ἄφεσιν 'he has sent me to proclaim liberty to the captives' Lk 4:18. In Lk 4:18 αἰχμάλωτος occurs on two levels: (1) in the literal sense of 'being a captive of war' and (2) in the broader sense of referring to all those who are oppressed by foreign domination.

The key words in that phrase are "foreign domination." To ignore Roman occupation would be to do a grave injustice to the text and its contextual meaning. The Israelites were dominated and oppressed by strict laws that were handed down from Caesar. They were ill-treated in their own land by foreign occupants. Richard Cassidy says, "In referring to Jesus' social and political stance, our intention is to emphasize that Jesus responded not only to the social situation of the poor, the infirm, and the oppressed, but also to the policies and practices of the political leaders of his time." They were literally prisoners of war in their own land. They are forced to live under the oppressive hand of the Roman government, and they cannot break free.

The goal of the text is to "recover sight to the blind." If we are to interpret this text as we have in the past as work that Jesus will do literally and spiritually, then it is safe to assume that Jesus is opening eyes to expose injustice. Throughout the Gospel of Luke he writes about instances when Jesus actually gave sight to those that were blind. "Go and tell John what you have seen and heard: the blind receive their sight, the lame walk, lepers are cleansed, and the deaf hear, the dead are raised up, the poor have good news preached to them. And blessed is he who takes no offense at me (Luke 7:22-23)."

William Hendrikson argues that "recovery of the sight to the blind" should not be exegete independently from "to set at liberty those who are oppressed." As the Lukan account records the fact that Jesus is reading from the scroll of Isaiah, he adds "recovery of sight to the blind" to the text. Isaiah does not mention that phrase. Hendricks reconciles to the phrases, the transition from one idea—the opening of the prison—to the other—the recovery of sight—is then explained by pointing out that when men bound in dark dungeons are set free, they again see the light of day, and in that sense their eyes are opened." He is stressing the idea that a part of Jesus' mission is to recover or give back the twenty-twenty vision to those that have been trapped. A renewal of mind, body, and soul brings them to a level consciousness that speaks to the ills of society.

Scholars attribute "to set at liberty those who are oppressed" to Isaiah 58:6. In its context Isaiah tells Israel these words, "Is this not the fast that I have chosen: To loose the bonds of wickedness, To undo the heavy burdens, To let the oppressed go free, And that you break every yoke? The oppression that Isaiah speaks of gives us the impression of individuals who are being crushed or mashed like a grape. Isaiah points out the fact that God is not interested in their rituals or festivals of false piety. He is more encouraged about what you do for others. Jesus reads this text before the people because Pharisees and Sadducees exalted the traditions of men over the commands of God (Mark 7:8).

Fasting and following religious rituals will not manipulate God into showing favor. He is more concerned with the motivation of the heart than the outward act. Oppressing the poor and weak of society and burdening them with slavery are the opposite of what they should be doing. God's desire for social justice is a familiar theme in the prophets, especially the book of Amos.

Jesus carries over this message from Isaiah because he is intentional about deliverance and freedom for the poor and disenfranchised. He not only physically releases them, but he offers a spiritual uplifting through his preaching and ministering. The "IVP Commentary" refers to it as, "Being under demonic oppression is like being trapped in a prison of pain and despair. Jesus offers release from such pain and dark despair. This is what his miracles picture and point to, the reality beyond the act of the miracle (11:14-23)." He brings hope and salvation to a people that have had their backs against the wall. Jesus is known and seen as the great liberator.

Jesus is the fulfillment of God's longing to have "someone intervene" by bringing justice into the earth. The radicality of Jesus' words and intentions have not gone unnoticed: the fact that the word for "poor" denotes a class identity: that the "prisoners" are those unjustly imprisoned, including the many political prisoners Rome kept in hell holes and those reduced to debt because of economic exploitation; that the "oppressed" cannot but refer to the people of Judea and Galilee who were oppressed by the crushing weight of the Roman Empire.

He provides them with previews of the work that He shall implement during his short walk on earth. By referring to the Isaiah, the fifty-eighth chapter, Jesus is alluding to the fact that Israel has not lived up to his mission. They have failed each other by not fulfilling what God required of them.

Jesus then tells them it is "time to proclaim the acceptable year of the Lord." These words are reminiscent of the jubilee year. This is God's year to act. The Jubilee Year always came with the liberation and emancipation of slaves. It was also a time in which all debts were cancelled (Lev. 25). In the book the Biblical Jubilee and the Struggle for Life it states:

'To let the oppressed go free,' should be interpreted not only in terms of the specific SabbathJubilee mandate to free the Israelite slaves but also in the larger sense of developing a social reality within which the conditions leading to slavery through debts and loss of land would be reversed. Similarly, we may suggest that 'the acceptable year of the Lord' or 'the year of the Lords' favor' that Jesus proclaimed as the coming of God's reign was no longer strictly one year in seven or one year in fifty but a new age of perpetual liberty for all God's people from every kind of oppression.

It is not definite if the year that Jesus spoke was actually a jubilee year, but it is clear that the listeners knew explicitly what Jesus meant when He said those words. Craig Keener says: "That Luke ends the quote on a note of salvation is probably intentional, but his readers who know Scripture well would know how the passage continues (speaking of judgment)." Jesus came to restore the whole mind, body, and soul of the individual. Jubilee was a pardon for all people, but especially it was a remembrance for those that 'had,' to help free those who did not 'have.' The jubilee had three main elements: liberty or release, restoration or return, and justice. Liberty means, "Do not control or use other people. Set them free." Restoration includes "returning land to its family, and people to their land." Justice means "fairness when calculating the price for a temporary sale." Charles Bradford refers to this passage of scripture as a type of authentic liberation theology. He says, "The Messiah Jesus came preaching an authentic theology of liberation. The message of Jesus, both radical and revolutionary, promised freedom to the nations—totals freedom. He makes the Sabbath the sign of his liberation and independence." Jesus promises to those his listeners as he reads from a Messianic passage that He is the Messiah that will restore and make all things new.

The goal is to see people restored to being what God created them to be: people who understand that they are created in the image of God with the gifts, abilities, and capacity to make decisions and to effect change in the world around them; and people who steward their lives, communities, resources, and relationships in order to bring glory to God. These things tend to happen in highly relational, processfocused ministries more than in impersonal, productfocused ministries.

Only through Jesus can this sort of restoration be made through building relationships and advocacy, then true freedom be obtained (John 8:36; Gal. 5:1; Col 1:13, 14).

THE (NEIGHBOR)HOOD

8

It is evident that from both texts we see restoration and renewal from two figureheads that have compassion and concern for the marginalized. Nehemiah which is seen more as a political figure versus a spiritual leader puts himself in harm's way to rebuild the wall in Jerusalem. Jesus, on the other hand, embodies not just a spiritual role, but a political role in His work that was done on earth.

It was discovered that both of these men were in a position to provide something that their listeners needed so desperately, which was hope. Nehemiah engages King Artaxerxes to return to Jerusalem to rebuild the walls. His motive for doing it is because the walls have been burnt down, and this is the place where his ancestors' graves are ruined. Nehemiah is familiar and knows about the rich heritage that his ancestors have left for him. Clearly, he was taught these things from an early age. He feels that it his mission and responsibility to do something.

Nehemiah represents those who do not live in the area of ruins, and yet they feel compelled to go help restore. All too often pastors and members have lost sense of responsibility for those that are marginalized. Assumptions are developed from various perspectives including experience as a pastor. When a person does not have a solid education of his or her rich heritage, he or she can suffer because of the lack of knowledge, and false information can enter into the mainstream mindset. The theology within the Adventist church has been a theology that has divorced the rich history of the African presence in the Bible.

Dr. Lester McCorn acknowledges that this problem is not simply within the Adventist, but there is a problem within the black church. He says: "Many Black Churches have become indifferent, if not hostile, to the persons who dwell in the very neighborhoods in which their edifices are located. The church should be a necessary ally and agent of liberation for poor, struggling, and fractured families." With the absence of the African presence comes a lack of concern for the least of these. If ministers cannot use the Scriptures to identify themselves in the word, then they cannot use that same word to uplift others. As a result, churches reflect the attitudes and beliefs of the minister. Therefore, if that ethic is not within the minister's core, then we can only expect to see more churches that are apathetic towards the struggle.

My theology was void of the fact that there is no need for a social gospel. Instead, I and others were encouraged to only view the Scriptures in a spiritual sense rather than in a literal sense. Nehemiah is motivated to act out of a respect for his ancestry. Ministers and lay people should be motivated to act, because of their ancestry. Great people like Martin Luther King, Jr., Malcolm X, Adam Clayton Powell, Frederick Douglass, and W.E.B Dubois are just a few of those that have put themselves on the front lines so that others could enjoy the current liberties of today. There must be a theology in us that sees ourselves in them, and not only a theology that sees ourselves in them, but also a theology that humbles us so that we could learn from them as well.

The second part of Nehemiah's goal to rebuild the walls in Jerusalem was the fact that he used his position as a cupbearer to influence the king to grant permission to rebuild the walls. It is vital to realize that the rebuilding of the walls was much more significant than just erecting bricks. Rebuilding the walls meant to develop infrastructure and security for Jerusalem. Walls are always known to keep unwanted visitors from conquering and pillaging communities. By Nehemiah rebuilding the walls he is essentially developing a system for the children of Israel to have safety and structure. It is evident that in impoverished communities that the walls of safety and infrastructure have been destroyed. Since these walls are broken down, all manner of destructive forces has been forcing their way into the community. Impoverished communities are plagued with businesses that look only to keep poor people poor and to oppress them further. Examples of these businesses are fast food restaurants, liquor stores, pawn shops, payday, and car title loan shops. There is no safety and peace; these people develop their 'walls' in these communities and only take from the poor but never give back. Instead, we should be motivated to develop businesses that give back to our communities such as hospitals, housing, banks, and clinics.

Nehemiah also gave the people in the community jobs to help rebuild the walls. Although he faced opposition from those that were within the camp, yet he was still determined to proceed with the plan because he had gotten confirmation from God. Often times we allow that one voice to turn into a concerted effort to prevent progress. Nehemiah was driven by compassion to restore a community that had been destroyed. The research is designed to put a fire and concern in ministers to mobilize our parishioners to help restore and rebuild that which is broken. As pastors, preachers and teachers there is a responsibility to use the positions that God has given to us, to do the work for them. The expectation to serve those who have been marginalized should be fulfilled despite the fact that pastors, preachers, and teachers live within or outside of the destitute communities.

In the account of Jesus, we find embodied in His work the same as Nehemiah's. The Scripture told us that Jesus is returning to his hometown, Nazareth. Instead of overlooking his tiny village, Jesus knows and understands that it is most important that he visits them at the local synagogue. Nazareth wasn't a large city like the other more prominent ones, but that does not negate the fact that the inhabitants are not special. He stood up in the temple and read. As we discovered in the exegesis, that literacy was very low in poor communities. If you can imagine this, the act of Jesus standing up to read had to be empowering to those that were in the synagogue on that Sabbath day. Picture if you will, Jesus, a man who looks like us and who is where we are from, is not only reading scriptures, but He is explaining it so that they can understand.

Jesus in that text represents the second class of people who can contribute in the fight for justice and equality. He stands as one who is from the impoverished community. Instead of leaving the community to do work elsewhere, He circles back to Nazareth to announce His earthly work. He declares that the Spirit of God is upon him, in other words the Spirit of God has enabled Him to do this work. Like Nehemiah, Jesus is driven by God's Spirit. Jesus reads a messianic passage from the book of Isaiah 61:1, 2, and Isaiah 58:6. The message is counter-cultural because Jesus not only stands as a priest and king, but He is also prophetic. The passion of God is to do a work of justice because He understands the oppression that they are facing.

The message is to 'preach the gospel, release the captives, give sight to the blind, and set the oppressed free. All of which speak of social justice and political activism. Roman had strict sanctions upon Israel, which made them prisoners in their own land. Jesus comes to lift weight off of them through healing and teachings. Jesus made great strides and impact on the poor. He was disrupting the so-called order of things in Jerusalem. There were Jews who were in cahoots with the Romans who were making meaningful gains by working for them. Jesus preached from Isaiah as an indictment on the Israelites that were oppressing their own kinsmen, and that judgment has come upon them.

The jubilee had become something that was forgotten by the Jews, and Jesus reminds them of their roots. He ends his proclamation by saying, 'to proclaim the acceptable year of the Lord,' the jubilee had come, the freedom that you have been longing has finally arrived. The Jubilee in its core call for remission of debts, restoration of land, sabbatical rest for land and human beings, and release from economic slavery. Jesus shows us that justice is a major component of His work. Charity is awesome since it provides a band-aid for wounds, but justice, on the other hand, is the ointment that heals the wounds. The book To Serve this Present Age gives us a solid definition between charity and justice:

In contrast, justice seeks to maintain a system of equality without partiality. That is, it seeks right treatment. Unlike charity alone, justice is not limited to reacting in order to fulfill a material real need such as food. Justice seeks right systemic relationships from the get-go. That is, "social justice focuses on basic causes of oppression, inequity, and disenfranchisement. It seeks to change public policy and public priorities. It works to empower people to take initiatives in ways that are positive and constructive. The movement for social justice understands that oppressed people have strengths, skills, cultural assets, and the responsibility to act corporately for their own common good. Where charity is reactive to specific material needs, justice is more proactive, working for changes in systems that create such needs.

Often times when Jesus would heal an individual, He would tell them to go show themselves to the priests in the temple (Luke 5:14, Luke 17:14). The temple was known as the place where individuals who were sick were reinstated into citizenship. If you were not a citizen, you were cut off from life's basic necessities. Clearly, not only did Jesus heal people, but He gave them their voice back. He used His voice as their voice and sought no personal gain from them. It is also important to note that Jesus makes His proclamation on the Sabbath day, as a means to say that the Sabbath was created to serve others. The Jews had used the Sabbath as an excuse to exclude themselves from the poor with their religious shows.

The Sabbath points to the fact that victims celebrate God's triumph in the midst of their struggle against injustice and evil. The Sabbath does not happen at the end of the week only but transpires with our deep awareness of God's presence in trouble. In this sense, the Sabbath is not a particular day, but rather awareness.

Jesus shows that the Sabbath is inclusive, and not exclusive. It was a day in which all were to be equal, and that we ought to be moved to help those who cannot help themselves. For the Pharisees and Sadducees the Sabbath became the most burdensome day of the week. They would fast and walk around in sackcloth as a means to show their religious piety. Not only were they putting on these so-called religious rituals, they were also using the temple as a means to exploit and take from the poor. We read in the Gospels, of Jesus overturning the tables and then inviting the blind and the lame inside for healing (Matt. 21:14).

Jesus and Nehemiah both offer exactly what is needed in many communities today, including the immediate context. That is a push to see, to remember, to restore, and to rebuild. not only walls, but to rebuild lives. They both represent individuals that sought to make the world a better place for others and not simply for themselves. If clergy and parishioners would find within themselves a theology that is concerned about "the least of these that are amongst us," it would break the cycle of allowing others to come in and conquer us and our people. Our churches are in some of the most decrepit and debilitated neighborhoods, but yet we are comfortable in erecting these fabulous houses of worship that will only serve ourselves. We are too complacent when it comes to driving past shops of exploitations and then driving back home. We must seek to end it by any means possible. The power that was available to Nehemiah and Jesus is the same power that is available to us as well. Nehemiah and Jesus used prayer, and the Spirit of God was unleashed for them. The Spirit was unleashed because they wanted to use the power from God to help others. Until a selfish motive is removed from our hearts, then we will begin to see that change that is so desperately needed in our world.

REMEMBERING THE WAYMARKS

9

One of the most defining moments in U.S. history was the Civil Rights Movement. During that movement the covers of racism were stripped off of social mores; and people, once having lived on the margins of society fought for equality. Many black religious leaders and church members were actively involved in the fight for justice, yet there remained plenty of religious organizations that did not want to be involved. Using Scripture to rationalize their position, they remained dormant and docile during the fight for fairness, equal opportunities, and justice.

The Adventist church organization did not choose to be quiet or neutral, but it has been documented that many ministers were vocal about not getting involved with marches or anything political. The understanding of this non-involvement has to arise from a faulty theology that stems from a "God will take care of all things" thinking. This type of theology has been ingrained within the fabric of the Seventh-day Adventist church from the pews and even into the classrooms. There were some black ministers who did march, and who did speak up, against injustice, but many of those incidents have gone undocumented. The Adventist church as a worldwide body has always tried to appear neutral in political affairs.

Although in recent years things have drastically changed, and more Adventist ministers have become more vocal, but there is still a lot of work to do. With the boom of the Internet age, and the easy access to information it has pushed some ministers, predominantly black to be vocal about injustice. The untimely deaths of Danroy Henry, Oscar Grant, Trayvon Martin, Eric Garner, Michael Brown, and Jordan Davis has pushed a younger generation to not being quiet. Recent elections have invited and motivated younger Adventists to be more actively involved in politics with the recent elections. From witnessing America elect its first African- American President to living through the Bush era as well as being products of Reaganomics, then to be alive to see the election of Donald

Trump, have spawned a turning of the tide towards a consciousness of a social justice gospel as well as ministries.

The framework of this chapter will explore the roots of the Seventh-day Adventist Movement and the era in which they came into existence. The integration and segregation had a lot of influence on the structure of this church. Early Seventh-day Adventist (SDA) church pioneers were products of their environment, which framed the ideas for their thoughts and views of the Scriptures. A faulty foundation leads to a faulty interpretation of the texts, and thus produces faulty rhetoric from the pulpit.

The basis of this chapter focuses on the lack of involvement the Adventist church as a denomination has during moments of civil crisis in America, and it particularly focuses on those that are victims of injustice and are forced to live on the fringes of society. Most ministers within the denomination either don't know or despise a liberation theology. We have one school that is a Historically Black College or University (HBCU), but yet still that school does not have a black theology or social justice curriculum. While there are classes on prophecy, and some instances and references to liberation theology, there is a voice when it comes to prophetic preaching that speaks truth to power.

Though stated earlier that more ministers are becoming vocal about acts of justice and treating people's' needs as holy, the overarching theology of the church and organization does not support or adhere to social justice or anything political. The body is comfortable with a theology that believes that Jesus will fix all things when He returns; until then, we must deal heavily with proclaiming preaching that is concerned with looking to the future instead of seeing the problems in the present. This phenomenon is not unique only to the Adventist church, but there are other major church bodies that believe these same ideas.

Historically, before church members were officially called Adventists, they were simply just followers of the principles of William Miller and the Millerites. William Miller was a Baptist preacher in the mid-nineteenth century. His desire for studying and learning the Scriptures was ignited during the rise of the second Great Awakening circa 1790-1820. During this time William Miller began to examine his life and question his existence through a careful evaluation and study of the Scriptures. According to George Knight,

His method of Bible study was to compare scripture with scripture in a methodical manner. 'I commenced with Genesis,' Miller wrote, 'and read verse by verse, proceeding no faster than the meaning of the several passages should be so unfolded, as to leave me free from embarrassment.... Whenever I found anything obscure, my practice was to compare it with all collateral passages; and by the help of CRUDEN's Bible concordance], I examined all the texts of Scripture in which were found any of the prominent words contained in any obscure portion. Then by letting every word have its proper bearing on the subject of the text, if my view of it harmonized with every collateral passage in the Bible, it ceased to be a difficulty' (A&D 6).

William Miller's study lead him to the book of Daniel, particularly verse 8:14: "Unto two thousand and three hundred days; then shall the sanctuary be cleansed." Miller adopted the "day-year" principle according to the interpretation of Numbers 14:34 and Ezekiel 4:5, 6. A day equals a year according to Bible prophecy, so that means that the 2300 days in Daniel 8:14 are really 2300 years before the sanctuary is cleansed. Through his studies, Miller determined that the decree given by King Artaxerxes to rebuild and restore Jerusalem in 457 B.C. (Ezra 7:1-27) was the beginning of the 2300 hundred days. When you add 2300 days (years), to 457 B.C. it will bring you to the year 1843. Miller, as well as others, believed that Christ would return in 1843.

This conviction led William Miller and many other preachers to evangelize and tell the world about the soon return of Jesus Christ. They created a newsletter called the Midnight Cry, in connection with preaching campaigns to wake up New York City about the coming judgment upon the earth. The return of Jesus would be known as the advent, the Millerites adopted the name "Millerite Adventists." Unfortunately, as history showed us Christ did not return in the autumn of 1843. Unwilling to relent on his theory, Miller and some others continued to study, and was convicted that Christ would return the Fall of 1844. The exact date was October 22, 1844.

On that day, thousands of believers in William Miller's teachings eagerly waited in great expectation for the advent of Jesus Christ. Even some dissenters and doubters were amongst the crowd, waiting to see if the Millerites' calculations had been correct. Before the approaching of the day, many believers sold their homes and gave up their wealth because they believed they would not need them anymore. To their dismay, the day came and went and Christ did not return. The day would be known throughout history as "The Great Disappointment." After that event most of the Millerite Adventists parted ways and began to start their lives over. Others, although disappointed and dismayed, continued to study the Scriptures. They still believed that something monumental did occur on October 22, 1844. Eventually, they came to believe that what had actually happened on that day was that Jesus Christ moved from the Holy Place to the Most Holy Place in the heavenly sanctuary. A gentleman by the name of Hiram Edson, who was also a Millerite, had a vision which led him to believe that the sanctuary in Daniel 8:14 was not the earthly sanctuary, but the heavenly sanctuary. The book A Brief History of the Seventh-day Adventists, says: "The new understanding of the cleansing of the sanctuary became a primary building block in the development of what would become Seventh-day Adventist theology. Coupled with the doctrine that the Seventh day Sabbath is a binding covenant between God and His children, they acknowledge themselves as sound biblical adherents to the Word of God. Thus, their name reflects and represents their beliefs, "Seventh-day Adventists."

Since it started with this small group of believers in 1863, Adventists prefer to think of themselves as a movement—a church that has never been stagnant but continues to be very doctrine-based. The church puts great emphasis on understanding the interpretation of prophetic texts, especially those found in Daniel and Revelation which point to the eminent return of Jesus Christ and His Kingdom. One of the major components of Adventist teaching is found is the three angels' message found in Revelation 14:6-12:

Then I saw another angel flying in the midst of heaven, having the everlasting gospel to preach to those who dwell on the earth to every nation, tribe, tongue, and people—saying with a loud voice, "Fear God and give glory to Him, for the hour of His judgment has come; and worship Him who made heaven and earth, the sea and springs of water. And another angel followed, saying, "Babylon is fallen, is fallen, that great city, because she has made all nations drink of the wine of the wrath of her fornication." Then a third angel followed them, saying with a loud voice, "If anyone worships the beast and his image, and receives his mark on his forehead or on his hand, he himself shall also drink of the wine of the wrath of God, which is poured out full strength into the cup of His indignation. He shall be tormented with fire and brimstone in the presence of the holy angels and in the presence of the Lamb. And the smoke of their torment ascends forever and ever; and they have no rest day or night, who worship the beast and his image, and whoever receives the mark of his name." Here is the patience of the saints; here are those who keep the commandments of God and the faith of Jesus.

Adventist eschatology looks at verse six as a reference to the Fourth Commandment which reminds the reader of God as the Creator of the Sabbath day. Verses nine and eight are a call to God's people to come out of Babylon. Babylon should be interpreted as living, thinking, and worship that is outside of God's intentions for His creation. Adventists believe that the issue found within this text is centered on worship and allegiance. The first angel calls Christians to worship God; the second and third angels tell the readers not to "worship the beast and its image." This text is a war on seventh day Sabbath worship, which God instituted at creation. It sees that the Sabbath will be the testing truth for the world for those that recognize it and for those that do not.

The church points to Roman Catholicism as the prime candidate that fits within verses eight and nine. The angel proclaims that, "Babylon is fallen...because she made all nations drink of the wine of her fornication." This fornication has been the Catholic churches' doctrines, which convinced the world that Sunday is God's day of rest and worship. Those that have adhered to it are drunk with her false teachings. Thus, by not only coming out of her, but by leaving Sunday worship, signifies a "sobering up," that brings clarity in regards to last day events.

Adventists also understand this text to be the union of church and state. In prophetic language, they believe that the "beast of the earth" found in Revelations is America, which will join hands with the Catholic Church and mandate that all people should worship on Sunday. Those that do not acknowledge the sanctity of Sunday will be persecuted. This idea is supported in Revelation 14:12, where John says, "Here is the patience of the saints, here are those that keep the commandments of God and the patience of Jesus Christ." The New Living Translation interprets the same text as "This means that God's holy people must endure persecution patiently, obeying His commands and maintaining their faith in Jesus. Adventists believe that the covenant that God gave to Adam and Eve at creation and was reiterated at Mt. Sinai is still binding today. They differentiate between the moral law and ceremonial law. To Adventists the ceremonial law was nailed to the cross, meanwhile the moral law still stands today. The Sabbath is the one commandment that is overlooked or ignored. All the other nine laws are recognized worldwide, but the Fourth Commandment has either been cut or removed from the fabric of Christianity. Adventists pride themselves as being Sabbath day worshippers, and a commandment-keeping people.

As well as being a bible-believing group, the Adventists believe in the gift of prophecy. That gift which has been defined and exemplified through Ellen G. White. The church acknowledges her as a prophet, whom God gave specific visions and knowledge to guide the church in these last days. Her works are constantly referred to for counsel and instruction. Some Adventists have strayed from her writings because there are a few who have trumped her teachings over the word of God. Some Adventists use her to abuse others as well as giving her the final say in regards to pertinent matters versus allowing God's word to lead. True Adventism understands that the writings of Ellen White are simply like the lesser light that leads to the greater light. Now there are many more layers to the Adventist message, which would cause us diversion. There are some misconceptions about the Adventist church in regards to its theology. Often times people tend to view Adventists as legalistic worshippers like the Jews, which is an easy concept to grasp because of the perception of some Adventist. The overarching body of the church knows that laws cannot save an individual, and that only comes through faith in Jesus Christ.

The church also recognizes that it has a duty to serve, help, reach, and teach the world about having a saving relationship with Jesus Christ. Although they recognize that the Sabbath day is a call to rest; it does not evade them from their civic duties towards the wellbeing of mankind.

Since its birth in 1863, the Adventist church has become one of the fastest-growing denominations in the world. Amazingly, the Adventists have churches on every continent. They have a humanitarian relief agency that caters to the needs of people all over the world: A.D.R.A. (Adventist Development and Relief Agency). The ADRA operates by going into poverty stricken areas including disaster-stricken areas to restore, to rebuild, and to provide ongoing support in the communities they serve. As far as numbers go, the Adventists are growing in leaps and bounds overseas because of their humanitarian efforts, but in North America the numbers are declining.

The one fact that remains true is that the Adventist church grew out of strong biblical interpretation amongst whites, and other African-American churches grew influence through preaching to blacks, which gave them a strong presence during the Civil Rights Movement. In most periodicals or books the Seventhday Adventist name isn't mentioned because it did not have an education or a theology for the oppressed. True "Christian education itself is constantly influenced by the historical, experiential, educational, cultural, social, political, and economic views of the community, and by those who teach." Primarily Adventist theology has always focused on the past and the future with little to do with the events transpiring today. "The purpose of Christian education is to provide biblically based programs, resources, and support within the church and community that will meet the needs, transform lives, and prepare individuals for every good Christian service." Therefore, the teachings of the Adventist church have always been and will always be "God will fix all things in the future." This type of teaching results in an apathetic view of fighting for civil liberties for all people. Samuel London Jr. says that Adventists adopted a 'sectarian ecclesiology.' "Sectarian ecclesiology, the belief that Christians should not conform to the secular world, also influenced the denomination's stance on politics? In expectation of Christ's imminent return, Millerites regarded political involvement as a secular activity that distracts Christians from their spiritual development. Furthermore, they were of the opinion that Christ's Second Coming coincides with the eradication of worldly government, which makes political activism pointless." He goes on to say, "Adventist leaders admonished members not to become involved in political affairs. Raymond Cottrell (1912-2003), a Seventh-day Adventist minister and associate editor of the Review and Herald (the official periodical of the church), condemned clerical participation in the 1963 March on Washington for Jobs and Freedom." His statement exemplifies Adventism's opposition to political involvement. Commenting on this political demonstration, Cottrell declared: "When the church appeals to the strong arm of the state to enforce its opinions by law, it goes far beyond the example and the commission of its Founder. It abdicates its Heaven-appointed task and takes up a work God never gave it to do." In the meantime, while other churches were organizing and planning to work together, Adventists were concerned about deciphering current events that only related to their own doctrine of eschatology.

As the Adventist church grew through evangelism, preaching and seminars, a vision was given to Ellen G. White in regards to the work that must be done amongst people of color. There is a book entitled The Southern Work which gives instruction in regards to work that needs to be done to reach African

Americans. It was during the 1890's that this awareness came to the forefront. Although there were some black Northerners who attached themselves to the Adventists, there were lots of work to do in the South. According to London, "In 1894 James Edson White (1849-1928), James and Ellen White's second son, assembled a missionary team with the purpose of helping improve the plight of blacks residing in the state of Mississippi." Because black education was frowned upon by Southern White Conservatives, blacks were not allowed to get proper education. During the Jim Crow era, blacks in America were not grafted into the mainframe of society. Instead, beatings and lynching's were at an all-time high. Those early Adventist reformers were intentional about opening schools of literacy that taught reading, writing, and mathematics to African Americans so they could function in a dysfunctional society that never embraced their presence. While they were teaching African Americans to read and write, Adventists also began to teach them through the Scriptures. This made other denominations angry because they were also converting their black students to Adventism in the process.

The year of 1896 was a pivotal year for Adventism's work with African Americans. During that year the Adventist church organization agreed to purchase a 360-acre plantation in Huntsville, Alabama for eight thousand dollars. Oakwood Industrial School would become Oakwood University. Since its genesis, Oakwood has trained and taught some of the greatest African- American leaders of the Adventist church. Currently, Oakwood is still the only primarily African American Adventist institution of higher learning in the world.

Yet, in spite of the opening of the first African American institution, race relations were not where they were supposed to be in the Adventist church. The first two presidents of Oakwood were

Caucasian. Even though the number of black Adventists had increased, they were viewed as inadequate to lead. Since Adventists were a product of the society upon which they were established; it felt right to them that a Caucasian be the director of the school. Discriminatory acts were performed at this Christian institution. With all white faculty and staff, racial slurs were common place, and it was even alleged that the president's son pointed his finger at some students working in a field and said, "These are all my daddy's niggers."

This led to the student protest in 1931. A small group of students known as the "Excelsior Society" rose up to challenge the all-white faculty and president, and the "separation of races" culture was adopted by Oakwood Junior College. "By the late 1920s and early 1930s, some students started complaining about the conditions at the school, calling it a "plantation" because of the heavy work schedules, low wages, and the inability to accumulate academic credit due to the workloads." Students also protested the fact that they did not want the vocational training that was spearheaded by Booker T. Washington but preferred an education more like the "The Talented Ten" that W.E.B Dubois proposed. The Oakwood protest was not unique; other African-American students were holding protests of their own. Knoxville College in Tennessee and Alabama's Talladega College were just a few campuses where there were student revolts.

The students' protests would not go unrecognized as they made their demands known to the General Conference; they were granted their first African American president, James L. Moran. White Adventist leaders were very reluctant with the appointment of Moran, classifying him as someone who was not fit to lead the campus. To their surprise, under the leadership of President J. L. Moran, student morale and enrollment increased. The school also saw its prominence and status rise; they advanced from being a junior college to a senior college in 1944.

The change at Oakwood amassed a collection of students who wanted more: students who desired to have leadership positions within the church and leadership roles in society. The school cultivated an environment that was conducive to teaching and equipping young minds with the fortitude to stand erect in a world infected with racism. Some of the greatest leaders of the church once attended Oakwood including Warren S. Banfield Jr., who was a president of the Tampa chapter for the NAACP.

Banfield's commitment to integration and social justice came from his personal experiences with racism. When visiting white Adventist churches, he had to sit on the back row or in the balcony. At the close of an evangelistic series, Banfield asked one of the denomination's white churches if he could use their baptistery to baptize African-American converts. The church refused his request because they did not want blacks to defile their place of worship.

Other prominent leaders are: Wintley Phipps, who is the Founder and CEO of the Dream Academy in Columbia, MD; Charles Joseph, former president of the Lake Region Conference of SDA and former pastor of the historic Stratford Memorial SDA Church in Chicago, IL; and Edward Earl Cleveland, who organized a NAACP chapter for the students of Oakwood. Even though he is known for being a great speaker and evangelist, Elder Cleveland was also a drum major for justice.

Simultaneously, the year 1944 was also important for Seventh-day Adventists because of an incident that involved an African-American woman named Lucille Byard. She was a devout Seventh-day Adventist who gave all her support to the denomination. Lucille became ill, and she only wanted to go to an Adventist hospital. Lucille and her husband took the train from New York to Washington to be served at the

Washington Adventist Hospital. To Mr. Byard's dismay, although he had called prior and made the proper arrangements, when they arrived at the hospital, things began to change. When the hospital discovered that Lucille Byard was an African American, a white administrator ordered that Mrs. Byard be rolled out into the hallway next to the exit. Mr. Byard, unaware and puzzled by the actions of the hospital, inquired about the situation. A white administrator informed him that Washington Sanitarium was strictly for whites and would not treat his colored wife. Although he informed the administrator that they were Adventists, the hospital still refused to offer her treatment. Mr. and Mrs. Byard ended up having to phone the Freedman's Hospital at Howard

University, which catered to black people. Subsequently, upon arrival at Freedman's Hospital, Lucille Byard's condition worsened because of the cold wintery night coupled with the fact that Washington University Hospital did not give her any blankets. Surprised and hurt by what happened, Mrs. Byard eventually died from pneumonia. Her condition could have been treated if she had been given the proper attention at the Washington Sanitarium.

The death of Mrs. Byard became the catalyst for black Adventists to fight for leadership within the church. While Oakwood students were rallying for a black college president, black Adventist leaders were rallying for their own conferences and organizations. Until that time, it was believed that blacks were not equipped to lead, so that's why whites were always, and in some cases still hold major positions within the denomination. Mrs. Byard's funeral was held at the historic Ephesus SDA Church in Harlem, NYC. Her funeral brought together many lay activists, and thirteen ministers eulogized her. The funeral spurred the formation of a committee for the Advancement of the Worldwide Work among Colored Seventh-Day

Adventists. This committee compiled a list of demands and requests that would be made known at the next General Conference Session.

Those two demands were either integration or the creation of black regional conferences, which would give African Americans more leverage in dealing with the issues of blacks in America. With a fight, white Adventist leaders finally decided to allow blacks to establish conferences that catered to the black community. Currently the black conferences in our denomination are called Regional Conferences; the white conferences are called State Conferences. There is a movement today, which is trying to eliminate regional and state conferences to come under one umbrella, but some Adventists are contending that regional conferences still need to exist. It is evident from the historical nature of the denomination that, if regional conferences are dispelled, then a major part of the church's history may also be eradicated. There are many graduates who have a rich history and have impacted society in the Adventist community. One graduate who matriculated through Oakwood was Charles S. Dudley. Born and raised in South Bend, Indiana, Mr. Dudley came from a strong Adventist background. Charles Dudley attended Oakwood College in 1943; upon graduating from Oakwood, he pastored many churches in the lower United States. Alabama, Mississippi, Tennessee, Louisiana, and Texas are just to name a few of the states. He was also the president of the South Central Conference of Seventh Day Adventists which is a regional conference. As the president of the South Central Conference, he oversaw the churches that existed in the states of Mississippi, Alabama, Kentucky, Tennessee, and Florida west of the Apalachicola. The headquarters offices are in Nashville, Tennessee.

As an adult and child, race relations during Dudley's life were laced with racial tension. Dudley's first encounter with racial justice came in 1947 when he took a group of students to an Adventist youth congress. Samuel London Jr. reports that as they were on their way to their destination, they decided to stop to order refreshments from an ice cream stand. A worker at the ice cream parlor told them that they were to stand by the black waiting stand. While waiting at the stand, the students realized that they were not being served. One of the students acknowledged that they were not being served; the host finally brought out ice cream, milkshakes, and floats. Dudley told the students not to touch any of the items. They did not pay for the items and left the establishment. Charles Dudley acknowledges this as his first encounter with racism. This experience shaped his entire life in regards to his faith and how he interpreted scriptures.

Charles Dudley also had the privilege of being a contemporary of Theodore Roosevelt; Mason Howard who was a black Adventist physician and civil rights activist was often referred to as the Black Maverick, T.R.M. Howard attended Oakwood Junior College. After Oakwood Junior College, Howard attended the Union College in Lincoln, Nebraska. He was the only black student at the school. From Union College he attended the College of Medical Evangelists, which is now known as Loma Linda University where he obtained his medical degree.

Howard first reached national prominence in 1955 when he became involved in the Emmett Till affair. Till was a black 14-year-old who, after supposedly flirting with a white woman, was murdered and then thrown into a river. Howard, who lived near the town where Till was killed, turned his home into a "black command center" for reporters, witnesses, and investigators searching for evidence. Although the two men charged with Till's murder were acquitted, Howard continued to speak out for civil rights and relocated to Chicago after receiving death threats for his role in the Till case.

Dudley credits Howard's fight for justice and to the struggle to improve the lives of those on the margins as the foundation, for the focus of his own ministry. Dudley went on to contend with the "powers that be" within the church to improve race relations amongst its black and white members. During a General Conference session, he along with a group under the direction of Frank W. Hale Jr. and his assistant Mylas Martin IV, protested the refusal of Mount Vernon Academy, an Adventist school, to admit black students. They also demanded that the General Conference select a black person to be among its ranking officials. As a result of this, delegates at the session elected Frank L. Peterson (1893-1969), an African American, to serve as vice-president of the General Conference of Seventh-day Adventists.

Dudley continued to be a drum major for justice within the Adventist church. Dudley protested against the white Huntsville SDA Church after they refused to allow two black students to enter their church service. He also supported a group of Adventists who chose to sue the denomination for not allowing black students to attend any of their academies. Elder Dudley also played a role in the Poor People's Campaign, which was the creation of Martin Luther King, Jr. After Dr. King's assassination his friend Ralph Abernathy kept the dream alive. In full support of demonstrators attending the event, Dudley sent a medical van to offer aid to any of the protestors. Dudley then received a message requesting his presence at the headquarters. "On Dudley's arrival, white Adventist officials asked him what he was doing in Washington, and why South Central's medical van was in the nation's capital. Before he could answer, the white leadership posed a rhetorical question that implied that the black conferences were no longer useful to the denomination. They then proceeded to accuse him of practicing the Social Gospel."

Dudley realized that the gospel is social and that he had a moral duty to support his own people. He acknowledged the fact that, whether Adventist or not, those individuals marching were his brothers and sisters. Once again, the denomination wanted to quell the voice and action of its African-American members. Dudley's support of the demonstration resulted in the federal government awarding the South Central Conference with $50,000 to do research on the condition of African Americans in Mississippi. Elder Dudley continued to be an activist and a social justice drum major. Dudley says, "My concept is that you ask the Lord to help you do your thing for your people. The white folk in the Adventist Church are worse than those outside the church. Racism still exists in the denomination, albeit in a subtle way." This statement reflects a current reality in the Adventist church although he made his statement over thirty years ago. There is still separation and bigotry within the Adventist church. The statement that racism still exists in a subtle way is accurate.

Elder Dudley was not the only social justice activist in the Adventist denomination. There were many more before him and many more after him. As long as racism has existed in America, there have always been groups of members and leaders who have fought to make the world better for others. Those 'others' are not simply the ones that belong to this church, but anyone who has been "voiceless" and needed someone to speak on their behalf.

The one common thread that was discovered between Charles Dudley and others who fought for equality is that their mutual experiences growing up in America shaped their consciousness for activism. Growing up in poverty, racism, and segregation gave them the fuel to realize that justice was worth the fight. None of these activists sat in classrooms where they learned about social justice from a biblical perspective. Instead, they acquired their knowledge and drive through contact and observation.

Oakwood University was the arena where many students, during and before the civil rights movement, protested against the status quo. The sad reality is that today's students do not have an opportunity to learn the names or stories of these individuals. There is no "black liberation" or "social justice" educational track for the theology majors. Adventist students in all denominations learn about Adventist history but not black Adventist history. That history is almost forgotten and hidden within the archives. As a product of Adventist education from elementary to grad school, these pioneers were not mentioned in my educational experience. It is possible that these stories were mentioned in some of the other institutions, but it is quite shameful that Adventists students in our traditionally historical black university spend four years without any education of their history within the church. Many Adventists grow up with the knowledge that Adventist pioneers had no involvement with the civil rights movement or that we were also a very passive denomination that was simply going to wait on the Lord to fix all things.

This chapter provides a fresh outlook on the roots of black Adventism within the denomination. We are living in a time of civil unrest, and if our schools are producing black theology majors who are divorced from their history, then we will produce church members who are divorced from the principle of giving back to those who have nothing. "Education is that whole system of human training within and without the school house walls, which molds and develops man." Adventist should learn about these great leaders from the denominations' church history, whether or not they attend Oakwood or any other institution.

Teaching the truth about the history is not for the purposes of inciting hate or producing a group of bitter Adventists. Instead, it should bring a level of appreciation for those who have contributed greatly to this great denomination.

The demonstrations and protests by Oakwood College students in the 1930's and the1960's dispel the myth that African-American Seventh-day Adventists conformed to and accepted social injustice within or outside the denomination. More importantly, the conservatism within the denomination did not immobilize African-American students. The actions taken by students in the past can serve as precedents for contemporary Oakwood College students who wish to organize or participate in social movements to end racial bigotry, sexism, and social injustice.

It is clear that agitation and activism is a part of the cultural, social, and religious legacy for African

American students at Oakwood College. According to one Oakwood student from the 1960s, "Adventist young people must be educated by the legacy of those who sacrificed to join the civil rights struggle as well as those who did not take the risk." In other words, young Seventh-day Adventists need to be educated and informed about the actions of Oakwood College students of the 1930's and 1960's and how they "altered the nature of race relations within the institutional structures of the SDA church."

Without this knowledge there results a miseducation of the Adventist. The Adventist young man or woman from Oakwood (particularly theology majors) leaves school with no idea that he or she graduated from an institution that started a movement within the denomination. Oakwood University is the home of black Adventists who did not conform to the rules of society, but instead sought to make things right. These young graduates will leave their school to serve in churches that are in predominant African American communities, but they will not know how to respond to the injustice they see in those communities. They will not possess inner fortitude or acumen to join civic unions or organizations that fight for equality and justice for all. Their sermons may not address life's vicissitudes. Instead they may be flabby and flaccid with limited spiritual depth. Thus, as a result of this miseducation, there will only result in misinformed members about their reality and responsibilities to not only themselves but to their neighbors and neighborhoods in which they serve. With the lack of historical education it may result in a level of stagnation of their level of effectiveness within the marketplace.

ME-OLOGY vs. WE-OLOGY THEOLOGY

10

The Merriam-Webster's Dictionary defines 'theology' as "the study of religious faith, practice, and experience: The study of God and God's relation to the world." The theological beliefs of the Seventh-day Adventists church are based on eschatology that ignores the present ills of society. Their belief is that, when Christ returns to Earth, all the present ills of society will be corrected. Thus, church members have an apathetic view of social justice. Seventh-day Adventists observe the seventh day of the week as the Sabbath based on the Fourth Commandment found in Exodus 20:8-11. They view the Sabbath as the ultimate seal of God and believe that observance of the day will be the testing point of fealty to the law of God. Seventh-day Sabbath observance creates a divide between Adventists and other Christian denominations. The comparison of Adventist theology, modern theological writings, and ideology will be made. Writings such as James Cone's Liberation Theology, Jorgen Moltmann's Theology of Hope, and essays from Liberation Eschatology by Margaret Farley and Serene Jones will be evaluated. All of these theologians present compelling arguments that have provided a renewed outlook on Sabbath observance and the study of lastday events. My conclusion is that we must learn; we must not 'wait to liberate' but to 'liberate while we wait.'

The concept of Me-Ology vs. We-Ology has to do with how we interpret the Scriptures. Does theology reflect more of a personal view versus a communal view? Most of the contemporary song that are sung during our services have plenty to do with what the Lord has done for me or what the Lord will do for me instead of what the Lord has done for us, or what He will do for you. Please do not take these words as my saying that we should ignore what God has done for us. It's important to always acknowledge and give thanks for all of our blessings from the Almighty God. One must take into consideration that there needs to be a balance in regards to our social commitment and responsibility to the least of these, and what are the ways that I can use the blessings of God upon me to help those that who are not as fortunate.

A We-Ologist understands that God opens avenues for me so that I can open it for others. They realize that true nature and work of Jesus on earth was solely driven to redeem and reclaim mankind from the oppressive and abusive hand of Satan. It does not refer to the poor as 'those people' but realizes that all of us in some way are poor ourselves. They see themselves as a part of the redemptive work that God wants to manifest through them.

Throughout its history, most Seventh-day Adventist churches have never created socially conscious programs that address civic affairs. Instead the church membership operates from the sidelines and gives play-by-play reports of current events. This behavior is the norm in the Seventh-day Adventist denomination. I attribute this lack of interest in social justice to their theology about last day events, which enables separatism, idealism, and even elitism.

Seventh-day Adventists pride themselves on the belief that they are the only denomination that has the truth. However, other Christian denominations feel the same way about their own core beliefs. Because Adventists hold this position about themselves, they adopt an "us" versus "them" attitude. They believe that they are the ones who have been chosen to call people "out of darkness and into God's marvelous light." The core of SDA theology is based on two passages of scripture: the Fourth Commandment in Exodus 20 and also the third angel's message in Revelation 14:6-7 which says:

And I saw another angel fly in the midst of heaven, having the everlasting gospel to preach unto them that dwell on the earth, and to every nation, and kindred, and tongue and people. Saying with a loud voice, Fear God, and give glory to him; for the hour of his judgment is come; and worship him that made heaven, and earth, and the sea, and the fountains of waters.

Adventists are convinced that this third angel is calling for the world to remember the Exodus Sabbath commandment and observe God's holy day of worship. They draw a parallel between the passage in Revelation and the Fourth Commandment because the angel in Revelation mentions the One who created the earth, sea, and the fountains. In the Fourth Commandment of Exodus, God is credited with "creating the earth, the sea, and all that in them is." Further, the verse in Exodus indicates that God "rested on the seventh day and hallowed it." Since the first angel in Revelation is drawing the listeners back to "worship," Adventist theology believes that the pivotal issue in the last days of earth will center on the observance of the Seventh-day Sabbath mentioned in Exodus.

The issue is not with the eschatology of the SDA church, but with the fact that they have missed the liberating factor of the Sabbath, and they don't understand that Revelation was written for an audience that was being oppressed by Roman occupation and domination. If there is a group of people who should be engaged in social justice reform, it should be the Seventh-day Adventists. It is the belief of this researcher that Adventist should "liberate while we wait" and not "wait to liberate." I could not agree with this statement any more:

It is not enough for the church to sit on a corner with a well-kept building while the community around it has so many needs. The church ought to be concerned about the saving of souls, but the church must understand that there are other factors that can hinder one's well-being in a spiritual sense as well. We are to be sensitive to the needs of the person beyond spiritual salvation.

Although some black Adventist churches are making strides in the area of social justice and speaking truth to power, most churches are still inactive due to the belief that God will fix all things when He comes back. Raphael G. Warnock addresses this phenomenon in black churches in his work The Divided Mind of the Black Church. He says:

As an instrument of salvation through Jesus Christ, is the mission of the black church to save souls or to transform the social order? Or is it both? As it would seek to be faithful to the gospel message and mission of Jesus Christ, is it called to be an evangelical church or a liberationist church? Can it truly be an evangelical church without also being a liberationist church? Can it be a liberationist church without also being an evangelical church? Put another way, does the gospel mandate insist that the church organize its institutional life so as to address itself primarily to "the slavery of sin" or to "the sin of slavery?"

Keri Day also questions the identity of the black church in her book 'Unfinished Business,' "The Black Church in the twenty-first century has become less clearly tied to its hallmark connection to social justice, reflecting increasing complexity and ambiguity. Sometimes it continues to stand within the traditions of social justice, while at other times the focus tends to be on individual prosperity and away from broader social transformation." Therefore, the problem will be discussed from a biblical perspective within this chapter. It will provide the basis for the thesis as well as create a foundation for the Seventh-day Adventist church to become socially engaged and politically involved.

In the preface of James Cone's book Black Liberation Theology he states, "I tried to uncover the wrongheadedness of the white way of doing theology and then attempted to set Christian theology on the right path of liberation." As indicated by Cone, we as a people interpret the Scriptures from a privileged point of view. There's no denying that whites have had a wide-reaching scope of influence in this world. Many of the major influential literary works and ideologies have been formed from their point of view, and others have been trained to study the Bible and use commentaries by the same population that used scripture to justify slavery. There is a proverb that says, "Until the lion has his own historian, the hunter will always be the hero." The lion has never had an opportunity to tell his side of the story and neither has the person of African descent. If the oppressor is the one who writes the history books and commentaries, then the oppressor can erase the facts and position themselves in the best light. Most blacks cannot identify the African presence in the Scriptures. I have even conversed with young people who had no idea that Egypt is located in Africa. Moreover, there are some in the black population who believe that the 'Curse of Ham' is the reason why Africans are suffering worldwide. If we approach the Scripture with a faulty foundation, then subsequent ideologies will be faulty as well.

The Moody Handbook of Theology defines theology in this by stating, "Theology comes from the Greek words theos, meaning, God,' and logos, meaning 'word'; hence, is a word or discussion about God." Theology is normally taken in a broad sense to signify the entire scope of Christian doctrines. Sometimes it is also used as a shortened form of theology proper, the expression used to signify the study of the Godhead. James Cone further states,

"There can be no Christian theology that is not identified unreservedly with those who are humiliated and abused. In fact, theology ceases to be a theology of the gospel when it fails to arise out of the community of the oppressed. For it is impossible to speak of the God of Israelite history, who is the God revealed in Jesus Christ, without recognizing that God is the God of and for those who labor and are overladen.

Black Liberation Theology acknowledges that God is actively involved in the affairs of the oppressed and marginalized. Not only is God actively involved, but God is also connected to them. He is not a God that only sits high and looks low. He is a God who has stepped down and revealed His presence here on earth to free His children from bondage. If God is righteous, then God must also be just, because righteousness and justice are synonymous. Therefore, God is the embodiment of justice. James Evans says:

To attempt to formulate an understanding of God's revelation apart from an analysis of the unjust structures of social existence does violence to both the significance of that revelation and to the integrity of the liberation struggles carried on by the victims of society. Such a separation would make God's revelation a quaint addition to our knowledge of an ancient religion with no salvific significance for the world in which we live. It would also distort the transcendent dimension of the universal human longing for freedom and justice.

Mr. Evans makes a clear distinction that any attempt to understand God's revelation apart from learning to understand human suffering and unjust structures is to do violence to the interpretation of Scriptures. Traditionally, the black Adventist church has found every way to divorce itself from the oppressed, downtrodden, and marginalized. It is disheartening to see that we have found ways to biblically justify isolating ourselves from oppressed populations and developing an attitude that says that they must pull themselves up by their own bootstraps. It is no wonder that we missed the liberating component of the Sabbath Covenant that God entrusted to the children of Israel at Mt. Sinai. In Deuteronomy 5:15, God tells Israel, "And remember that you were a slave in the land of Egypt, and the Lord your God brought you out from there by a mighty hand and by an outstretched arm; therefore, the Lord your God commanded you to keep the Sabbath day. The Sabbath is the great equalizer. God initiated the Sabbath and the Jubilee year as a means to invite those on the margins to rest and find freedom. Walter Brueggemann says, "It is no stretch at all to see that on the Sabbath day these vulnerable, exposed neighbors shall be 'like you," peaceably at rest." The Sabbath is not merely a sign to God's covenant people in the last days, but it also stands as a memorial reminding us that, since we were once slaves, God expects us to break the chains of others in slavery and invite them into His rest.

According to James Cone:

There can be no Christian theology that is not identified unreservedly with those who are humiliated and abused. In fact, theology ceases to be a theology of the gospel when it fails to arise out of the community of the oppressed. For it is impossible to speak of the God of Israelite history, who is the God revealed in Jesus Christ, without recognizing that God is the God of and for those who labor and are overladen.

It appears that Mr. Cone is arguing that it is impossible for the church and theologians to divorce from their frame of mind that God's primary concern is for those who labor and are overladen. The foundation of black theology must begin and end with the oppressed. Seeking the approval of organizations that look to crush the weak and defenseless cannot influence this foundation. Black Liberation Theology forces us to come out of our comfort zones and enter the "danger zone" where we seek every way possible to alleviate the pain and suffering of the downtrodden.

The task of Black Liberation Theology is to make Christianity really Christian by moving Black people with the spirit of black dignity and self-determination so that they can become what God intended them to be. Black Liberation Theology is a theology of community, and as such, it is opposed to any idea that alienates it from the Black community. And, since it seeks to interpret Black

Religion, Black Liberation Theology endeavors to de-construct the Christian tradition in view of the Black predicament and to destroy the influence of heretical White American Christianity.

Those who teach from the Scriptures must adhere to—and not ignore—the explicit theme found within the Bible that shows that God does not like oppression. Unfortunately, Adventist theological schools tend to minimize this fact. While they may acknowledge that there is suffering and pain in the Scriptures and the world, the emphasis remains on teaching that the liberation God performs today is spiritual and not physical. When Jesus took His stand in the temple in Luke the fourth chapter and said that He had been sent to set the captives free, give sight to the blind, give liberty to those who are oppressed, and proclaim the acceptable year of the Lord, Adventists acknowledge that as a spiritual liberation. A spiritual liberation is more of a metaphysical occurrence as opposed to a literal one. Black Liberation Theology says:

To suggest that he (God) was speaking of a "spiritual" liberation fails to take seriously Jesus' thoroughly Hebrew view of human nature. Entering into the kingdom of God means that Jesus himself becomes the ultimate loyalty of humankind, for he is the kingdom. This view of existence in the world has far-reaching implications for economic, political and social institutions. They can no longer have ultimate claim on human life; human beings are liberated and thus free to rebel against all powers that threaten human life.

Once again, when the Sabbath is viewed through the lens of the oppressed and downtrodden, we will begin to realize and discover the justice component found within it. If the Sabbath and Jubilee year are the great equalizers that God calls us to, and if the Sabbath is the core doctrinal piece of the Adventist church, then that same Sabbath should push us to move beyond rest on the seventh day. It must also seek for rest for those who are under the control of a cold system. Mr. Cone explains this concept even further:

In view of the biblical emphasis on liberation, it seems not only appropriate but necessary to define the Christian community as the community of the oppressed which joins Jesus Christ in his fight for the liberation of humankind. The task of theology, then, is to explicate the meaning of God's liberation activity so that those who labor under enslaving powers will see that the forces of liberation are the very activity of God. Christian theology is never just a rational study of the being of God. Rather it is a study of God's liberation activity in the world, God's activity in behalf of the oppressed.

If the most exalted Being in the universe, God, is connected to the weak, then those that profess to have faith in Him must lock arms with Him and fight for their local communities. Nehemiah's faith in God expresses this concept. Nehemiah could not sit back and be complacent in the palace while his people were suffering. Instead, he gave up the luxuries of palace life to rebuild the walls in Jerusalem. He identified himself with the community in Jerusalem based on his connection with God and his connection with his heritage. "Theology by contrast cannot be separated from the community which it represents. It assumes that truth has been given to the community at the moment of its birth." Jesus exemplifies this connection through His life on earth and His declarative message found in Luke 4:16-19. The church has failed to view itself in this light. The church organization as well as each individual who professes faith in God must identify with those who suffer. James Cone says:

Theology is the continued attempt of the community to define in every generation its reason for being in the world. A community that does not analyze its reason for being in the world. A community that does not analyze its existence theologically is a community that does not care what it says or does. It is a community with no identity.

Black Liberation Theology is mainly concerned with its connection with the community and ensuring that those around us are lifted. It does not seek to patronize oppressors. Instead, it will—at any cost— fight for those who cannot fight for themselves and be a voice for the voiceless. It views Scripture as the blueprint to alleviate anguish, hurt, and pain. It shows that "black" pain is God's pain. Walter Brueggemann explores and expands the idea of what the community needs; he says:

I have tried to say that prophetic ministry does not consist of spectacular acts of social crusading or of abrasive measures of indignation. Rather, prophetic ministry consists of offering an alternative perception of reality and in letting people see their own history in the light of God's freedom and his will for justice. The issues of God's freedom and his will for justice are not always and need not be expressed primarily in the big issues of the day. They can be discerned wherever people try to live together and show concern for their shared future and identity.

Without Black Liberation Theology, God becomes a caricature who has gone to prepare a place for us and will only help us when He is ready to return. It projects an image of a father who has a child that is being abused but tells the child not to worry because one day he will return and fix the problem. In the meantime, the child continues to bear the abuse. If the child cries out against the abuse, the father only gives him or her encouraging words and tells them to wait for their coming reward. It seems strange that the father would not do something to alleviate the suffering immediately. In a real sense, many people have this view of God. To them, He is a Father who sees the abuse that His children face every day but holds off from helping them while He prepares their new home. When preachers perpetuate this idea of God, they encourage the chasm between people and God to widen. It provides a foundation for people to believe that faith in God is only spiritual anesthesia to numb the pain but provides no cure.

Black Liberation Theology forces one to address the problem found in mainstream theology that disregards the black condition.

The appearance of black theology on the American scene then is due primarily to the failure of white religionists to relate the gospel of Jesus to the pain of being black in a white racist society. It arises from the need of blacks to liberate themselves from white oppressors. Black theology is a theology of liberation because it is a theology which arises from an identification with the oppressed blacks of America, seeking to interpret the gospel of Jesus in the light of the black condition. It believes that the liberation of the black community is God's liberation.

Most theologians tend to turn away from Cone's Black Liberation Theology because they perceive it as only addressing the issues found within Black America while ignoring other populations that suffer. Cone addresses this notion by saying, "The focus on blackness does not mean that only blacks suffer as victims in a racist society, but that blackness is an ontological symbol and a visible reality which best describes what oppression means in America." Therefore, in the context of this work, 'black' or 'blackness' should not be limited to color but must also be widened to include all those who share the same experience as underprivileged Black Americans. The ill treatment of Mexicans and El Salvadorians in America could also be defined in terms of the 'black experience.' The persecution of the Native Americans—and the annual celebration of Columbus Day—is a reminder of America's proud exploitation of the Native American. Blackness according to James Cone, "then stands for all victims of oppression who realize that the survival of their humanity is bound up with liberation from whiteness." Therefore, Black Liberation Theology is concerned with survival of all populations under harsh conditions.

Black Liberation Theology is also confrontational because its duty is to call out the sins of America. It calls for us to acknowledge slavery as one of the cruelest and heinous acts committed against any group of people. The black church has remained quiet on the political front—claiming religious piety as its basis— but the silence makes it seem as if we are complicit in the acts of oppression both within our ranks and in society.

Some would argue that Black Liberation Theology puts heavy emphasis on the present and minimizes the ultimate liberating event of the return of Jesus Christ. Thus, we must examine how Black Liberation Theology relates to Revelation and eschatology. James Cone says:

Revelation is God's self-disclosure to humankind in the context of liberation. To know God is to know God's work of liberation in behalf of the oppressed. God's revelation means liberation in behalf of the oppressed. God's revelation means liberation, an emancipation from death-dealing political, economic, and social structures of society. This is the essence of biblical revelation.

The root of the word Revelation means 'reveal.' The book of Revelation is about God revealing His plan for an oppressed people. One must take into consideration that the book of Revelation was written by John the Apostle on the isle of Patmos.

Patmos served as a prison to any person that spoke against Roman occupation and oppression. John wrote this epistle from a prisoner's perspective. In Revelation, John wrote that Jesus visited him while he was imprisoned on Patmos. This gives further evidence that God is actively involved in the lives of the marginalized. When Jesus visited John, He gave a revelatory message that shows His plan for the redemption of mankind. The way that John illustrated this message used imagery to remind Jewish readers of what the Babylonians did to their ancestors. Adventists only view Revelation's Babylon in context of the Catholic Church, but that limited thinking narrows the scope and power of the Word of God. Babylon represents any entity or system that is outside of God's will for humankind. For that reason, Babylon not only represents Rome but also Jim Crow laws, "three strikes" policies, and tax laws that favor only the rich. In context, Revelation is a book about hope and freedom in Christ's return, but it does not negate the fact that we must liberate while we wait for ultimate justice to be exercised.

The famous theologian and scholar Jürgen Moltmann says:

Eschatology means the doctrine of the Christian hope, which embraces both the object hoped for and also the hope inspired by it. From first to last, and not merely in the epilogue, Christianity is eschatology, is hope, forward looking and forward moving, and therefore also forward looking and forward moving, and therefore also revolutionizing and transforming the present.

He is arguing that eschatology must not only be limited to last day events, but its message and idea must be intertwined with the matters concerning the world today. Eschatology helps us understand the 'last day,' but it also calls us to look at conditions 'today.' "Eschatology should not be it's [sic] end, but its beginning."

Some argue that Moltmann's Theology of Hope supports the idea that humans must anticipate a future of peace whilst suffering. This is not what Moltmann meant. Moltmann defines hope in the context that, when Jesus came to earth and dwelled amongst men, women, and children, this was the beginning of eschatology and last day events. The presence of Jesus being actively involved in the lives of the marginalized and performing acts of liberation signifies that Jesus was giving them a meaningful outlook on their dismal situations. Suffering human beings don't have to continue with every day suffering—they can enjoy life while they wait on the advent of Jesus Christ. Moltmann says, "Hope makes us ready to bear the 'cross of the present'. It can hold to what is dead, and hope for the unexpected. It can approve of movement and be glad of history." He goes on further to say:

It pronounces the poor blessed, receives the weary and heavy laden, the humbled and wronged, the hungry and the dying because it perceives the parousia of the kingdom for them. Expectation makes life good, for in expectation man can accept his whole present and find joy not only in its joy but also in its sorrow, and happiness not only in its happiness but also in its pain.

To hope does not mean to know the future but rather to be open, in an attitude of spiritual childhood to accepting it as a gift. But this gift is accepted in the negation of injustice, in the protest against trampled human rights, and in the struggle for peace and fellowship.

Moltmann's Theology of Hope and Cone's Black Liberation Theology share some of the same values. Both theologies acknowledge God's active work in the lives of those who suffer. The black church is God's agent in the community, so it must live out the gospel. When the power of the Holy Spirit resides in the body of Christ, the church should be motivated to live out God's heart and character exemplified by the work it does in the community. The church cannot be comfortable with the pain and suffering of others. According to Cone, we ought to rebel against unjust societal laws. This means that, as long as there is sin, the church should always contend with those who desire to maintain the status quo.

When discussing liberation eschatology, one cannot ignore the Sabbath covenant given to the children of Israel. As stated previously, the Sabbath is God's great equalizer. It is a moment in time when all of God's creation is called to rest from labor. There is social justice in the Sabbath. Jürgen Moltmann says, "All are meant to come to rest together. Moreover, because the Sabbath applies to all equally, all have the same right to rest on that day. The enjoyment of the same divine grace has as its corollary the equal rights of human beings and animals." Through the Sabbath, God is creating a community of the equal and free—a community that acknowledges that all of God's creation is equal. The Adventist community—strict Sabbath observers—must also understand that economic justice should be available for all people. The Sabbath covenant must be the impetus that transforms our communities. Jürgen Moltmann uses Acts 4:32-35 to support the idea of equality. During that time, possessions amongst the early believers all belonged to each other. The text says, "And so it turned out that not a person among them was needy. Those who owned fields or houses sold them and brought the price of the sale to the apostles and made an offering of it. The apostles then distributed it according to each person's need." Moltmann believes that, because the Israelites observed the Sabbath, it provided an equality of economics that was based upon the principle of "what is yours belongs to me, and what is mine belongs to you."

In a world in which the possessors are becoming ever richer and the have-nots are suffering more and more privation, a community that lives in solidarity like this really is the beginning of divine future that endures in a world of inequality—a world that will pass away because it has no permanent durability. It has no permanent durability because it is unjust.

Sabbath observers must realize that the core tenet of the Sabbath is not simply about rest, but it is God's way of declaring that we ought to be one. Therefore, if the community is doing badly, then we are doing badly as well. The implications of the Sabbath are to invite us into a covenant with our neighbors, acknowledging them as co-laborers in a world that looks to suppress the family by making it harder and harder just to survive. Adventists theology must make the community the center of its focus. This is even more important to the black church, since most of them are located in impoverished communities. It must not only view community members as individuals whom it seeks to convert and baptize. It must also seek to convert the community from the evil that is imbedded in it. Mr. Cone says:

In the New Testament the church (ecclesia) is the community that has received the Holy Spirit and is now ready to do what is necessary to live out the gospel. It is the assembly of those who have become heirs of the promises of God; and because they have experienced what that means for humanity, they cannot accept the world as it is. They must rebel against evil so all citizens may know that they do not have to behave according to unjust societal laws.

If the Holy Spirit is the compelling force that convicts us of all truth, then we must allow Him to help us see the community as not just our neighbors but also our family.

Mr. Cone lists three responsibilities of the black church in the community, which is worth discussing. "First, it proclaims the reality of divine liberation." The preaching of the gospel is the means by which the church verbally communicates God's heart and provides motivation to a dying world. It is through this avenue that the world will understand that God is not divorced from the affairs of the world but is actively involved in seeing things change for the better. For too long, the preached gospel has supported passivity towards social injustice. This type of message miserably fails to address the pain in this world with the solutions found in Scriptures.

Mr. Cone makes his next point by saying, "Secondly, the church not only proclaims the good news of freedom, it actively shares in the liberation struggle." While the church preaches good news of Jesus' liberation, it must also be actively engaged in the struggle for freedom. Even if the "powers that be" do not see the blatant disregard for the anguish of "the least of these," we must let the community know that we see their suffering, and we will not ignore it. "The church is the community that lives on the basis of the radical demands of the gospel by making the gospel message a social, economic, and political reality. It has the courage to take the risk, knowing that, at this early stage, it lives in a society that refuses to believe the gospel message. It, thus, goes against the grain of societal existence because its sole aim is to share with Jesus Christ in His liberating activity." Throughout the gospels, we witness Jesus' liberating activity in His work with and for the poor. In Matthew chapter 11, we read that after Jesus entered the temple and turned over the tables of the moneychangers, He made room for the blind and the lame, and He healed them. There are many instances in Scripture where Jesus sat and ate with publicans and sinners. In the book Ministry of Healing, author Ellen G. White says:

We are living in the midst of an "epidemic of crime," at which thoughtful, God-fearing men everywhere stand aghast. The corruption that prevails, it is beyond the power of the human pen to describe. Every day brings fresh revelations of political strife, bribery, and fraud. Every day brings its heart-sickening record of violence and lawlessness, of indifference to human suffering, of brutal, fiendish destruction of human life. Every day testifies to the increase of insanity, murder, and suicide...And while the world is filled with these evils, the gospel is too often presented in so indifferent a manner as to make but little impression upon the consciences or the lives of men. Everywhere there are hearts crying out for something which they have not...The world needs today what it needed nineteen hundred years ago--a revelation of Christ. A great work of reform is demanded, and it is only through the grace of Christ that the work of restoration, physical, mental, and spiritual, can be accomplished. Christ's method alone will give true success in reaching the people. The Saviour mingled with men as one who desired their good. He showed His sympathy for them, ministered to their needs, and won their confidence. Then He bade them, "Follow Me."

In this quote, White is saying that there is a need for a revolution of Christ, which will spark a revolution for change. She highlights that the Savior mingled with men. In other words, He took the time to relate with them and understand their plight whilst they were under the oppression of the Roman government. The message of Jesus Christ causes us to be advocates for the community that we are ministering to.

Mr. Cone's next point: "Thirdly, the church as a fellowship is a visible manifestation that the gospel is a reality." This statement is so important because the church runs the risk of becoming social ventriloquists instead of social activists. We are speaking the words of Jesus, but we are not doing the work of Jesus. To the community and the world we have become nothing but noise makers that speak flowery words but do nothing substantial to back them up. It is our duty to truly live out the gospel of Jesus and not make His teachings become detestable to man.

The social gospel had it right in that the gospel needs to be more than just a nod-to-God hour, one day a week. Faith needs to bear the fruit of action within a world full of alienation, apathy, and hurt. In fact, the term social gospel is a pleonasm since any gospel that is not social is not the gospel. God's covenant is with all creatures and all creation. Christ died to save not just "Me" but "We," not just souls but the entire created world. For there to be a new heaven and a new earth, the gospel message must be social.

Cone continues to stress this fact by saying, "If the church is not free, if it is a distorted representation of the irruption of God's kingdom, if it lives according to the old order (as it usually has), then no one will believe its message. If someone tells me that Christ has set us free from all alien loyalties, but he himself obeys the loyalties that he claims Christ has defeated, then I must conclude that he does not really believe what he says." When the church does not live up to its social calling, it becomes a contradiction and become criticized and ignored.

The words of James Cone and Jürgen Moltmann make it clear that eschatology and liberation are not two polar ideas. Instead the two concepts are intertwined. Adventists tend to isolate the two ideas or heavily depend upon eschatology to absolve themselves from acknowledging the suffering of human beings and relieving their pressure. If the City Temple SDA church wants to change from just being a church group that takes up space in the neighborhood, then it must accept Black Liberation Theology and the Theology of Hope as foundational pieces of their own theology. The account of Nehemiah reveals to us that although Nehemiah did not live in Jerusalem, he was still concerned about the needs of the city's inhabitants. Additionally, Luke's account of Jesus entering the temple—to proclaim the Jubilee year and also speak a message of liberation on the Sabbath day—informs us that Jesus was concerned about underprivileged populations.

The church cannot remain comfortable with doing just enough to ease the congregants' consciences. Black Liberation Theology reminds congregations of the unbreakable tie that they have with the community. Collectively, churches must actively push back the forces of evil affecting its residents. Jürgen Moltmann's Theology of Hope suggests that although we hope for a better and brighter tomorrow, humans can still enjoy some sort of peace whilst they hope for a future that is completely rid of suffering. It is through Moltmann's Theology of Hope that it is realized that churches must 'liberate while we wait.' That means it is the duty of the church to preach the true message of the gospel that fights against systems of oppression. Also, like Nehemiah, churches must help develop systems of infrastructure for the communities that are negatively affected by those systems of oppression.

Community involvement and organization pushes us to put the 'neighbor' back in the hood. For too long theology has afforded the opportunity to label impoverished communities as the "hood" or "ghetto." When referring to these communities in such manner, there is an indication that these inhabitants are not our neighbors, and this must change. When understanding that these people are our neighbors, we will be impassioned to seek the change that Black Liberation Theology talks about. Black Liberation Theology is unapologetically concerned about the plight of "black" people regardless of their nationality. Black Liberation Theology may scare some people because it is "black" and confrontational, but it is needed. Blacks and minorities in America have been taught to appease whites and not identify with anything that is too "black." That way of thinking has always led to the black church diminishing black suffering and adopting a "why can't we all just get along" attitude, which the oppressor loves because it does not hold them accountable. For that reason, the image of the black church has been marred in the community. As Cone states,

Black denominational churches seem to be content with things as they are, getting fat on the misery of their sisters and brothers. Although possessing the greatest potentiality for black revolution, the black churches satisfy themselves with white solutions to earthly injustice. That is why persons interested in justice in this world so often scorn the black church, saying that it is nothing but a second-rate oppressor.

The description could not have been more accurate. This is the image we project to the community. To them, our church is only a building that takes up space and—once a week—takes up all the extra parking. We have become broods of vipers who only seek to collect the widow's mite and use up resources without using any of it to help the local populace. There must be a change, but that change will only come when we understand the true revolutionary teachings of Jesus.

FOR THE SHALOM OF THE (NEIGHBOR)HOOD

11

The obvious reality is that many of our churches are in areas of what was once thriving and surviving. Today, the southern sector of Dallas is saturated with pawn shops, car title loan shops, and payday advance shops. It also has one of the greatest grocery gaps in the United States. As far as food is concerned, people in the community have to rely on processed food from local bodegas and fast food restaurants. It is a known fact that what you eat affects your thoughts and decision making. Abandoned buildings, condemned houses, and open fields full of trash are everywhere you go. In the middle of all this devastation stands the church, which is supposed to be the light in the midst of darkness.

The intention of this chapter is to pay careful attention to the factors that lead to what is commonly known as the 'hood' or the 'ghetto.' Gentrification, redlining, redistribution, and economic justice are some of the topics that will be discussed. Questions that will be addressed include, what are the overarching themes that make up a ghetto? Does the 'hood' have sponsors that ensure their existence and survival? What should an affluent church's responsibility be to the community, if there are any? It may very well appear that the church appears to be okay with the proliferation and destruction of the community, but that may not be the reality. The reality is that the church would like to do more to alleviate pain and suffering, but they do not have a praxis or methodology for engaging community. They may talk about the need to assist and to help, but it is merely a healthy conversation with no action. Using examples of other churches that have been successful with developing infrastructure, whilst being true to the prophetic message found in the Scriptures, will be most helpful in establishing a rule of thumb that, not only your church will use, but other churches in the Adventist denomination and outside.

Throughout the years it has been discovered that the problems facing the poor in America are not selfinduced issues. A lot of the ills of society are associated with policies that favor the rich, racism, and white supremacy. Ian Lopez describes the role of the government in Dog Whistle Politics. He says that the government has four important roles to play:

First, to help people weather the vicissitudes that easily plunge families into poverty, for instance job loss or ill health; second, to provide escalators of upward mobility, such as quality schooling, higher education, and mortgage assistance; third, to build the nation's infrastructure, thus laying the groundwork for the next great economic boom; and fourth, to rein in marketplace abuses through regulation, and to prevent excessive concentrations of wealth through progressive taxation.

It is quite evident that this is not the case. The poor appear to be getting poorer and rich continue to get richer. The country is divided into two groups: 'the have gots' and the 'the have nots.'

In spite of the societal challenges, most churches do a great job at ensuring that they turn on the lights twice a week: Wednesday nights for prayer meeting, and Saturdays for Sabbath morning worship. Regular church members and visitors would travel from as far as fifty miles away to attend the services. For years the church would invest in the things that they deemed most important. They viewed only the things that would benefit themselves as valuable. As Mr. James Josey describes this problem in his doctoral work, "The church today has a perceived value problem. If the unchurched are to be reached, then the problem of value must be addressed." If we truly value the unchurched, then it would shape our theology, programs, and ministries from an internal focus to an external one.

For this part of the book we will do a case study of Eddie Polite and his tenure as the senior pastor of the City Temple SDA Church. Pastor Eddie C. Polite has always been adamant about pushing the congregants to redirect the church from being self-serving. Lots of the funds that churches collect are often spent on special days and special meals. These 'special services' would often entail the invitation of a known speaker, and they included travel, hotel, car rental, and honorarium. Churches would also sponsor a meal for all of the visitors that attended on one of these 'special days.' Bothered by this behavior, which has gone on for years,

Pastor Polite along with the help of Pastor Furman Fordham developed and informed the church that he would spend the first five years of his tenure planning and implanting a new vision for the church. With prayer and careful study, he introduced what is known as a "Ministry Driven Module." The plan splits the church leaders and ministries into four quadrants: serve, share, connect, and grow. Certain departments fall under these various quadrants. For example, under the "share" ministries' quadrant, you would find these ministries: health and wellness team, community services team, social action team, and special needs team. The outcome of the quadrants is to engage the church departments to work in conjunction with each other under the auspices of reaching the community. The module finds its basis in the great commission given by Jesus to the disciples in Matthew 28:19, 20, "Go therefore and make disciples of all nations, baptizing them in the name of the Father and of the Son and of the Holy Spirit, and teaching them to obey everything that I have commanded you. And remember, I am with you always, to the end of the age." Jesus encourages His disciples to 'go' and to 'make disciples.' The making of the disciples has to be through community action.

When the church finally adopted the Mission Driven Module, Pastor Polite shifted his attention towards developing a center that could meet the needs of the community. The church reinstated it's 5013c and obtained grants to fund what is known as the Dallas City Temple LiveWell Center. The LiveWell Center is located in the Wynnewood Village plaza. The plaza is about ten minutes away from the church, and it serves the individuals in the community. The center has had some really good initiatives. They run a job fair for ex-convicts which has resulted in various companies coming to the center with job offers for those who have a conviction on their record. They have also done record repair classes which teach anyone who has been convicted of petty crimes how to have those crimes removed from their records. The LiveWell Center also offers classes on health, diet, and diabetes prevention. In the future the director of the center hopes to continue the initiatives that they have begun as well as t offer mental health counseling sessions.

It should be noted that some resistance came from, not only the church but the governing body of the City Temple Church which is the Southwest Region Conference. Issues in regards to liability, insurance, and salaries were some of the setbacks. Although all of these matters were answered in a presentation given to the officials, they still had some reluctance. In order for the LiveWell Center to attach the name "City Temple" to it, the pastor had to convince the board that it would start out as an entity to be independently funded and would not have to rely much on church offerings to carry it. To this day, it still operates as an entity that is fully funded through grant money, but the church acknowledges that grants are not a consistent stream of cash flow. So in between the occupying grants the church steps in and assists financially.

One of the reasons for the opposition towards the LiveWell Center is a result of Seventh-day Adventists not adapting or creating a theology that addresses the least of these. Like all Seventh-day Adventists, the theology focuses heavily on last day prophetic messages. If the LiveWell Center were a place where individuals could pick up materials regarding eschatology and doctrinal tenets of the Seventh-day Adventist church, individuals may have a stronger and more complete buy-in from the church; not only a complete buy-in, but also complete participation and acceptance. It is difficult for Adventists to see a prophetic last day 'end times' message given unless it is through preaching and doing Bible studies. The idea of eschatology through the lens of social justice is something absolutely unheard of and awkward. Since the Seventh-day Adventist organization has taken a hard-line stance against politics and truly stands by the notion of separation of church and state, they see the problems of society as a perpetual never-ending cycle that Jesus will ultimately end with the advent. The belief that we ought to stand by and watch people suffer until the day Jesus returns is absurd. The black Seventh-day Adventist church must take a hard stand in regards to its identity and mission. Frederick Harris emphatically raises this point, "After Emancipation, when newly freed black men had their first opportunities for open political engagement, religious institutions provided for the organizational infrastructure for mass political mobilization." "Thus, it was churches that provided meeting space for political gatherings, and church leadership and laity were elected to state political conventions and to state and local elected offices."

In the book Faith-Rooted Organizing it says, "Transforming a community requires more than neighborhood development; it demands courageous organizing and persistent strategic advocacy." Whilst organizing churches and leaders has its place in the work for a better society, advocacy ensures commitments from local politicians and leaders to effect change in the neighborhood. Both aspects require hard work and patience. It should also be noted that the work of reformation and change does not happen overnight. Opposition and resistance can come from the outside, and, at times, even from the inside, but the workers cannot allow those things to impede the progress that must be made. The church is in need of a consistent and persistent methodology by which it will transform the community that it is in. It is quite evident that if one were to take a drive through the southern sector of Dallas, one would see neighborhoods that have been devastated and abandoned. Various studies have been performed that shed light on the redlining that occurs in some districts which are predominantly black. These issues are not simply native to Dallas, but all across America the working poor are subject to the policies and machinations of the elite. Edward Goetz highlights this issue in New Deal Ruins: Race, Economic Justice, and Public Housing Policy, as he describes the problem with public housing:

Although public housing's political support had never been widespread or entirely secure, the shift in its clientele from "the deserving poor" (as represented by the intact families of working, albeit low-income residents) to marginalized single-parent, welfare, and minority families has meant consistent underfunding and a steady disinvestment, both literal and political, from the commitment to provide safe, decent, and affordable housing through public ownership. In too many places the physical stock was allowed to decay, and maintenance was deferred or ignored.

His analysis points to the fact that certain zip codes are intentionally left to be underfunded and destroyed because of their clientele. Public housing was never created to be an end-all for the residents; it was created to be a stepping stone for families to move on from.

Not only is there decay in the public housing sector, but we also find decay in the community. There are boarded up businesses with heaps of garbage stacked in front of them. The only new businesses that come to these poor areas are those that seek to exploit and hurt those who are already suffering. Examples of these businesses are payday loan advance shops, car title loan advance shops, and pawn shops. Food deserts are normal, as the only options for the residents to choose from are fast food chains, liquor stores, and Chinese cuisine. Claud Anderson describes some of the issues in the communities that many churches reside in:

We have more killings and crime, more school dropouts and drug users. Integration killed our communities. We have no black economic structure to solve the problems of our community. Our black churches and families are weak and struggling. We have yet to gain control of our communities and our destinies. The Vietnamese, Koreans, Indians, Iranians and Mexicans are putting up profitable businesses in our neighborhoods. And we are still hopelessly vulnerable to every danger—from police brutality to violence and poverty.

These are the conditions that so many people live in. These are the conditions that children have to walk past to get to their already failing school. The problem is that these issues are intentionally created as a means to gentrify struggling communities. Lance Freeman refers to gentrification as such: A definition supplied by the Encyclopedia of Housing defines gentrification as "The process by which central urban neighborhoods that have undergone disinvestments and economic decline experience a reversal, reinvestment, and the inmigration of a relatively well-off, middle- and upper middle-class population." Big banks, as well as major corporations and developers entertain the idea of destroying communities so that they could seize properties at basement prices. The process by which they redevelop is through building expensive condominiums and inviting a brand-new population to make the community better. With this new population comes police presence, supermarkets, better parks, and simply, an improved way of life. The major issue with this is that those that make the decisions on behalf of the 'hood' do not live in the 'hood' or anywhere near it. These decision makers represent the leeches of society that suck resources out of the 'hood' and pump them into their pockets. John Powell says, "Our aim therefore should be for universal goals and outcomes, not just universal processes or strategies. There are instances when universal processes or strategies can work, but there is also a need for targeted strategies for a specific purpose and outcome. Certain areas have certain demands and needs. Powell goes on to say, "Programs should be universal in goals, but, unless they are targeted in approach, the goals of fairness and inclusion will falter – not just for the most marginalized blacks and the undocumented, but also for many other racialized and non-racialized groups such as people living in rural areas, people with disabilities, and the elderly."

The one entity that continues to thrive and survive in poor communities is the church. The church has always and will always have a presence in the 'hood.' Robert Franklin states:

The black church has been and continues to function as the hub of civil society and remains the center of social life in many black communities. It was the community's source of aid and philanthropy, a center for learning and literacy, a zone for political education and mobilization, an organizer of financial capital, and keeper of a collective cultural memory.

It is from the church that all meaning for life and instruction should flow. God has called the church to be the light in the midst of darkness as well as an advocate for justice, not just for its members, but for the community wherein it resides. "For this reason, the preferential option for the poor not only demands that we seek to know, seriously and responsibly, the reality and the causes of poverty: not only does such an option lead us to make our pastoral action more effective and to deepen our theological reflection." The only way that this concept can become a reality is based upon the church's response to poverty and pain. If you were to exegete the community where your church is, or perhaps a zip code outside your neighborhood you would discover that there are visible, tangible effects of a community and people that have been abandoned. Although some critics may say that the members do not live on those streets, it is still an unreasonable excuse to seclude oneself from the problems they are facing.

Civil rights activist and theologian Dr. Robert Linthicum provides a praxis and methodology for churches that are seeking to engage their communities. His perspective comes from first-hand experience through his work in African-American communities and overseas. In the opening chapter of the book, Linthicum states that:

Most of the writers of the Bible were motivated by a perception of God's intentions for human society— not only spiritual, but also economic, political and social. The Bible paints a very clear picture of the way society is meant to be and a vision of the world toward which we should be powerfully working.

In most cases, the church only has an idea of what the world should be and how they would like it to operate. An idea is great, but the vision makes it plain and realistic. Having a biblical vision of the world allows the looker to see things the way God intended. It is through that vision that we are able to confront those systems of oppression. Because a church does not have a working social justice methodology, nor does the Adventist church organization, a foundation is very much needed to provide the change that is desperately desired.

The overarching question that has consistently presented itself is what does your church value? It appears that the church values evangelism and reaching the unsaved, but the majority of the funds are spent on themselves for special days and occasions. A shift must occur in the minds of the congregants and that should come from the pulpit. The church must see themselves as God's representatives on Earth. They must acknowledge themselves as God's instruments of righteousness and justice and the modern-day Israelites that He intended for them to be called out of darkness to be a light. Robert Linthicum says:

It is because Israel stands for a national justice and relational culture that is opposed to what the other nations stand for. And if Israel does not keep itself separate from those nations, it will eventually be seduced by those nations into forming a society equally committed to domination by the wealthy and powerful and devoid of a people truly right with God and each other.

It is the whole concept of being in the world but not of it. The church cannot adopt a capitalistic mindset that incorporates the ways of the world in its policies and procedures. I find all too often within my context that the congregants allow society to influence their thoughts and imaginations about the marginalized. These audacious thoughts allow the church to justify their actions by creating a separation with the community. They may talk, preach, quote scriptures and discuss methods of reaching those on the fringes of society. Unfortunately, it means nothing until we actually seek to make contact with them. Robert Franklin explains this idea further:

There are times when we should study the pain, and times when we should share and feel the pain. Then there are times we should mobilize to end the pain. But leaders who are unaware of, or uncomfortable with engaging and addressing, the pain of the people are unlikely to mobilize the power of the people. Underneath our pain lays our power. But someone must name our pain and guide us through the common pains and the occasional deeper traumas of human existence. There can be no impact unless there is contact.

Robert Linthicum believes that the church ought to seek the 'shalom' that the Scriptures speak of. Our understanding of 'shalom' cannot be limited to what we know as 'peace.' Shalom carries deeper and richer implications, and it should inform the way we think and look at society. Mr. Linthicum defines it as such:

Shalom is an exceedingly rich concept, a comprehensive word dealing with and covering all the relationships of daily life, expressing the ideal state of life in Israel and, indeed, the entire world. The concept of shalom essentially has to do with what the Israelites saw as being foundational to life: being in community with each other.

He explains further what that means for the Jews:

So, when Jews wish each other "shalom," they are wishing for each other's health, security, long life, prosperity, successful completion of an enterprise, victory in war. In other words, they are wishing God's best for the entirety of a person's life, for all her relationship with others, for all he sets his hand to do. And they are wishing for such fullness both for that person's life and for the Jewish community through the world.

This concept of shalom is a universal idea that speaks to the community. Linthicum emphasizes that Christians ought to seek the prosperity and peace of their neighbors. It is the responsibility of the church to ensure that all areas of lives are doing as well as they can. In order for true meaningful change to be ushered in, there must be community organizing. Nehemiah sought not only to rebuild the walls in Jerusalem, but he also created a sense of communal integrity amongst the Israelites.

The task of faith-based community organizing is not so much community development as it is community organizing. That is, the task of faith-based organizing is not, finally, to organize institutions to address their issues of public life, as it is to organize in order to create a community. A 'shalom' community is birthed in the city by moving beyond the continuing addressing of the people's issues.

The fabric of life must be a reality in the community that our church is in. The idea of 'shalom' is communicated to us in these verses found in Jeremiah 29:5-7:

Build houses and dwell in them; plant gardens and eat their fruit. Take wives and beget sons and daughters; and take wives for your sons and give your daughters to husbands, so that they may bear sons and daughters—that you may be increased there, and not diminished. And seek the peace of the city where I have caused you to be carried away captive and pray to the Lord for it; for in its peace you will have peace.

If we are to use Linthicum's interpretation of 'shalom' then it must be understood within this context that the success of Israel is dependent upon the success of the Babylonians. God encourages them to seek the 'shalom' of the city, for in its 'shalom' you will have 'shalom.' Linthicum stresses the fact that God is not requiring them to seek the peace of Jerusalem, but to seek the peace of the city that they are in, and that city is Babylon. God encourages Israel to pray for the success of those who have held them captive. The congregants of the church would not even imagine that their success is contingent upon the success of the inhabitants of their community. Therefore, if we are to apply the text, it is a fact that the church's stagnant, unproductive status is a result of their insular understandings of the Scriptures. When the church ceases from the continual self-seeking ways and puts aside its own agenda for the sake of others, then there will be results not only in the community, but in the church as well. The text has universal implications, which means that wherever the church is, then it ought to pray for the peace of that region. Israel was in Babylonian captivity for seventy years which ensured that they would model this behavior for their children. The seventy years of exile was enough time for a generation to die before Israel was freed. Ironically, a church can reside in a community for over fifty years, time which they cannot get back, but it is enough time to start modeling a ministry that reflects the interests of the community.

Linthicum provides the work towards 'shalom' in the city through being God's presence in the city, praying for the city, practicing your faith through action and proclaiming the good news. Each work provides a step-by-step action plan for engaging and transforming a community through God's righteousness, justice, and' shalom.' Linthicum says that, "we are to be advocates for the powerless. It is the job of God's people to 'stand in the breach' and defend the cause of the poor, the powerless, and the marginalized before the 'principalities and powers' of the city and state."

There are some critics within the Adventist organization that strongly stand against social justice. In an article written by Hilari Henriques of Prophesy Again entitled, "The Everlasting Gospel vs. the Social Gospel" she writes that the social gospel agenda clashes against the everlasting gospel mentioned in Revelation 14:6-12, which is a major foundational doctrine of the Seventh-day Adventist Church. Within the organization there has been a movement amongst younger Seventh-day Adventist pastors and local leaders to be more engaged in civil rights and advocates for the weak. Oakwood University, the only HBCU operated by the Seventh-day Adventist Church, recently held a march in the wake of the untimely deaths of unarmed young black men. Andrews University, which is also operated by the Seventh-day Adventist Church and also houses the only Adventist Theological Seminary, held a march as well with the university's co-chaplain and a group of students. The article pinpoints these happenings as distractions to the true mission God has called the church to. Henriques writes:

During these marches and protests, there has been no mention whatsoever of sin and righteousness and the only remedy for societal and institutional evils and abuses. Social reform and the acquisition of temporal benefits are meaningless if those being targeted, both the oppressed and the oppressor, are not led to repentance and heart conversion. Christ's truth is not uplifted and emphasized in these activities; therefore, such exercises are ineffective in achieving lasting change.

This misunderstanding of social justice is not just akin to her own thoughts. The article garnered 512 shares on Facebook, and over thirty-five comments in total support of the article. The thinking behind this article sheds light on the miseducation of Adventists when it comes to the Sabbath, social justice, and African American history in America. The author continues with an admonition to all Seventh-day Adventist pastors: "Seventh-Day Adventists pastors should be exposing this diabolical evil, the social gospel. Since this perversion of the gospel does not emphasize the three angels' messages, its adherents will be led to lay aside their peculiar doctrines and join in ecumenism with the various religions and churches of Babylon." Henriques fails to realize that the Book of Revelation was written by the Apostle John while he was incarcerated on the isle of Patmos. John is writing from a prisoner's perspective to Christians who were oppressed by Roman occupation and domination. This kind of thinking comes from years of Adventist doctrine that looks at Scripture through the eyes of the privileged and is only concerned with pushing their unique agenda on Earth.

Another article written by a Seventh-day Adventist entitled, "Social Justice, a Christian Duty," although not as brutally misinformed as the prior one as the author did support social justice, but the response was very 'Adventist.' The author asks a question and then proceeds to answer it:

So how do we fight for social justice without hurting our cause? The simplest way is to love. Love was the reason Jesus came to restore God's character to man. What had we misunderstood about His character? Simply that God is love. We can analyze it, dissect it, study it for hours on end, but the result will be the same: God is love. And if love is at the very root of His character, shouldn't it be at the root of ours?

Once again the words 'hurting our cause' are always an agenda within the church's motives. It seems like Seventh-day Adventist only exist to promote a last day message which entails the government mandating that all Christians worship on Sunday. Although all denominations have some sort of agenda that they want to push, Adventists see themselves as the only truth bearers left on Earth. Their total disregard for the sufferings of humankind is diametrically opposed to the gospel Jesus preached. Jesus' inaugural speech is found in Luke 4:16-19; His last message to the disciples can be found in Matthew 25:34-41:

Then the King will say to those on his right, 'Come, you who are blessed by my Father, inherit the Kingdom prepared for you from the creation of the world. For I was hungry, and you fed me. I was thirsty, and you gave me a drink. I was a stranger, and you invited me into your home. I was naked, and you gave me clothing. I was sick, and you cared for me. I was in prison, and you visited me. Then these righteous ones will reply, 'Lord, when did we ever see you hungry and feed you? Or thirsty and give you something to drink? Or a stranger and show you hospitality? Or naked and give you clothing? [39] When did we ever see you sick or in prison and visit you? And the King will say, 'I tell you the truth, when you did it to one of the least of these my brothers and sisters, you were doing it to me! Then the King will turn to those on the left and say, 'Away with you, you cursed ones, into the eternal fire prepared for the devil and his demons.

Jesus' final counsel to His disciples was to administer series to the 'least of these.' It is a call to ensure that those on the fringes of society are ministered to and cared for. For example, in the parable, Jesus tells those that ignore the poor to depart from Him because He did not know them.

The article does not definitively give instructions on how to seek justice for others. The author states that we must love because God is love. The statement is consistent with the general belief of the Adventist that 'Jesus will fix everything when He comes, so we are just to love the poor.' Once again, I cannot emphasize how much of a disservice we have done to ourselves by only focusing on a gospel that waits for the last day, whilst ignoring what happens today.

In conclusion, the works of Robert Linthicum and Robert Franklin will prove helpful in stating the case and the thesis for the project. Ultimately, the task is to show the discrepancies and holes in the Adventists' doctrines because there is a lack in regards to social justice ministries and advocacy.

The examples raised in this paper will provide the catalyst in proving ministries of social justice and advocacy work. For the church to adapt and adopt a methodology and praxis for the work of social justice, they need to see a working model of it. For most of the lives of those Adventist Church congregants, they have been exposed to only one aspect of the gospel. The failure to launch from theory to practice is a result of being kept in the dark, and it is a misrepresentation of the radical teachings of Jesus Christ. The foundational piece of this chapter is discovered in seeking the 'shalom' of the city that Linthicum encourages Christians to seek. The peace and prosperity of Israel is dependent on the success of the city. This does not mean that the Israelites must pray for continual oppression and systems that will push them off the edge of society; but it means that they ought to be the presence of God even as they are sojourners in the land until God brings them out.

The discussion about Sabbath as social justice will be able to debunk the myths and ideas that it is only a day of rest; but it is also a day of equality and favor for the disadvantaged. The observance of the Sabbath must be the means by which all Adventists should seek to civically engage in the affairs of society. God ensures through the Fourth Commandment that we ought to share Sabbath principles with the stranger that is within our gates as well as others within proximity. There is also the 'acceptable year of the Lord' that Jesus emphasized at the end of His sermon in the synagogue. The 'year of the Lord' refers to the Jubilee Year, which encompasses the freedom of slaves, but also sought justice for the earth in that the land was given an opportunity to rest. Sabbath implications and studies will help build a bridge between the church and social justice. Since the Sabbath is the major tenet of the church, all teachings and new ideas must be derived from its core message.

WHAT DID I DO?

12

The last few years have been quite a journey for me writing and implementing this project. It gave me the opportunity to learn more about myself and my context as it relates to the structure of the church and social justice. In this chapter of my document I hope to take you on this journey with me as I describe and analyze the results of the work done.

I led the church in a four-part preaching and teaching series entitled "Putting the Neighbor back in the Hood." The purpose of the sermon series was to enlighten the church about social justice through the Scriptures. The church must see it, to be it. Education and action hurt the church in many ways. The belief that charity is a social justice is a notion that must be debunked. Although charity is great, justice must not be ignored. Charity only puts Band-Aids on issues, but justice seeks to be the ointment that heals. Our Godgiven mandate is to help those who are the most vulnerable of society and provide them with the power to stand on their own two feet.

The sermons preached came from various texts in the Bible from the Old and New Testaments. A campaign and flyers were made, and the series opened with the message entitled "This is for the Thug in You," using Matthew 21:12-14 which says:

Jesus entered the Temple and began to drive out all the people buying and selling animals for sacrifice. He knocked over the tables of the money changers and the chairs of those selling doves. He said to them, "The Scriptures declare, 'My Temple will be called a house of prayer,' but you have turned it into a den of thieves!" The blind and the lame came to him in the Temple, and he healed them.

The interpretation of the text is to show that Jesus expressed anger and disappointment towards the religious leaders who were taking advantage of the poor. Jesus overturned the tables, and if we are to follow His examples, then we ought to overturn the tables of oppression that physically dominate the poor. The text then shows that Jesus invited the blind and the lame to come into the temple. He invited those that were living on the fringes of society. As Obery Hendricks states in his book The Politics of Jesus, Jesus used His anger for the mistreatment of others. The example Jesus provides in this account is the example the church should follow. City Temple was informed that there are things in this world that should make them angry, and that anger should drive them to make changes.

The second installment came from the story of the good Samaritan found in Luke 10:25-37, which draws its title from the passage itself, "Who Is My Neighbor?" The church had to grapple with the understanding that my neighbor is the one that I have been taught to overlook. The ongoing struggle and strife between the Jews and Samaritans provide a substantial basis for how we treat our neighbors. The media teaches us who to despise and who to project prejudice towards. Through the increasing number of negative images of African Americans put out by the media and the continual vilifying of Muslims, the body has gone to extreme measures to protect themselves from such individuals. The church was challenged to find ways to use their resources to help those that are in need. It was also made known that it is the duty of the church to make sure that the roads travelled by individuals are safe enough that they are not beat up and robbed by bandits.

The third installment of the preaching and teaching series was entitled "We Gonna Be Alright," a title extracted from Kendrick Lamar's blockbuster album 'To Pimp a Butterfly." During that week, we looked at the story of Joshua 8:1-2. Looking at that conquest of Israelites of Ai, the church was led to understand that the victory did not come without some challenges. In the previous chapter the Israelites could not defeat Ai because there was "sin in the camp." It was to their discovery that Achan had stolen goods from a previous battle and hid them underneath his tent. The primary focus of that sermon was the community or to take care of those that hurt the community within the community. Although we have a plethora of issues facing us from all angles, there is a social responsibly amongst ourselves to point out and call out the Achan's within our communities that halt progress. The point that must not be taken lightly is that Israel had to deal with the issue and not an outside party. Often in our community we wait for others to handle our situations, yet we are always disappointed by the way it is done. After Joshua sought the Lord, he confronted Achan. The Scriptures inform us that for them to move forward, they had purged the camp of Achan and his family through death. In no way were we advocating the murder of anyone, but the responsibility of the church is to address the issues within our community that are caused by those that are in it. We cannot be all right until we start taking a hard look at our community and ourselves.

The final installment of sermons was taken from the book of Luke 4:16-19, entitled "This is a Message from Our Sponsor." It was a deeper look into the revolutionary teachings of Jesus Christ when he entered the temple. Jesus intentionally made His way back to His home, Nazareth, to deliver a message about social change and the acceptable year of the Lord. Luke informed us that Jesus drew His message from the book of Isaiah. Jesus informed the listeners that the Spirit of the Lord was upon Him to preach the gospel to the poor, heal the brokenhearted, proclaim liberty to the captives, give sight to the blind, set at liberty those that were oppressed, and to proclaim the acceptable year of the Lord, which was also known as the Jubilee Year. The emphasis on the text passage plays an intricate role in the minds of Seventh-day Adventists because it highlights the fact that Jesus preached this on the Sabbath. He also correlated the ideas and concepts of social justice with the jubilee year found in Exodus 21:1, 2. The church was taught that the message Jesus proclaimed in the temple was not just spiritual ideas, but that Christ came to literally deliver the oppressed. Jesus spoke truth to power, because what He preached about was a reality.

For Adventists the Sabbath has been only marked by simply as a day of rest from all labors and cares. The rest that God intended was not to be something that was mutually exclusive that allows us to turn off ears to the suffering of mankind. It was brought to the acknowledgement of the church that Jesus' call to social action was a divine charge from God to be more actively involved in change.

The church's reception to the message was overwhelmingly positive. The congregants began to catch the vision, and, because of their desire to hear more social justice teachings, my ministry leaders and I developed a response card with a series of questions to get feedback. The questions were: Did you enjoy the series on social justice? Would you like to be more active in social justice? and Do you think that this church should be engaged in the affairs of the community? On that Sabbath, we collected about two hundred fifty cards from the congregants with each member desiring to have more knowledge in regards to what God says about social justice.

The cards were collected and put into a database with weekly emails being sent with social justice themes.   After the database was put together, I invited the Dallas Area Interfaith (DAI) to do a social justice training workshop. The DAI is a multiethnic and multiissue faith-based group that addresses social needs in the Dallas metropolitan area. The training was centered around the problems facing the people living in the Cedar Crest neighborhood where City Temple finds itself with lack of police response, stray dogs, prostitution, and poor lighting at the train station. Their presentation at the workshop also spoke about the pressures facing families and the corporations that make decisions on behalf of residents in Cedar Crest.

The presentation led to what was known as a community action night where local residents and other faith groups convened to voice their concerns. The theme of the evening was based in Nehemiah's plan to rebuild and restore the walls in Jerusalem. For the Saturday morning service before the action night, I preached about Nehemiah's passion to make a difference. Nehemiah left his position in the palace to go to the ruins to be with his people to build an infrastructure of safety and security. The appeal was made to congregants of City Temple to be present at the Cedar Crest Church of Christ as we voiced the concerns of the residents to city officials.

The purpose of the training and action night was to expose a dormant, commuter church to the concerns of the community. It also opened the church to discover the difference between social justice and charity. Charity would have been a temporary Band-Aid on the problems, but justice at times is long, tedious, and requires lots of patience. As a result of the community action night and collaborating with various faith groups, it sparked an excitement amongst the members of the City Temple church to be more cognizant of the problems and vigilant in fighting for justice.

Since this was a new venture for the City Temple Church, I found that the model of preaching and teaching was a great introduction to models of social justice. The initial steps of allowing them to discover God's active role in the liberty of His people confronted the members to reevaluate the way they viewed God and the Scriptures. The discovery of joining hands with others from different denominations proved to be extremely helpful as well. The ability to hear and see the pain that the residents were suffering from proved to them that the struggle for equality and freedom is real. I have discovered that the process of teaching and preaching does not work for a post-modern congregation. They are looking for real stories in real time and real work that they want to become engaged in.

Since the preaching of the sermonic series, the church has seen an influx of young adults seeking more and meaningful ways to express their faith by helping the disenfranchised. Although it galvanized the congregation and visitors to be more involved, I realized that preaching and a few cameo appearances in the community were not enough. The feedback that I received from some of the congregants was the usual comments, "Pastor, that was a great sermon," "thank you for that word," etc. It must be noted that on a regular Sabbath there were at least five hundred individuals in attendance; at the action night there were only about thirty people. As stated before, the congregation enjoyed the sermons; there were many that affirmed it by saying, "Amen," clapping their hands, pointing, and standing up. However, when their presence was expected and required: the shouters were absent; the clappers were silent; the pointers put their hands in their pockets, and the standers chose to sit in their homes. I imagined that these findings were only unique to my church, but the other denominations were facing the same thing as well. Although I was very disappointed by the turnout, I did leave the room for the simple fact that some people did not have the flexibility to be able to show up for the "Night Out" to address issues facing the community. I rested on a few conclusions mentally: either some members were too busy; some were too tired; or, perhaps, some were just uninterested.

As disappointed as I was, I continued to preach sermons with a social justice theme. The previous chapter provided the immediate positive feedback from the sermons. There was also feedback received that was not too negative, but it is so important that it cannot be ignored. Some members stated that the pastor preached too many social justice sermons. They stated that they wanted to hear more sermons about the mark of the beast and the Catholic Church. The congregants asked to please deal with weightier topics like Daniel and the Book of Revelation. Essentially, they were asking for more sermons about what makes us Adventists, and the true church, which goes back to the fact that there is a generation of Seventh-day Adventists that see traditional Adventist prophetic messages as the true gospel and enough for us to put our energy in. When it comes to prophetic messages in the Adventist church, that solely means sermons pointing to the works of the Catholic Church and how that relates to Adventists losing their freedom to worship on Saturday.

At times, it is very difficult for them to wrap their minds around the idea that a prophetic message does not have to solely deal with last day events. To the Adventist mind prophecy always refers to what pertains to the end times and the imminent return of Jesus Christ. A prophetic word always deals with the immediate matters at hand. When God gave the Children of Israel prophetic messages, it was not to simply point to the future, but it was primarily focused on them dealing with the crisis at hand. Through Micah, who is placed into the section of the minor prophets, reminds the Israelites in chapter 6:8, "No, O people, the Lord has told you what is good, and this is what he requires of you: to do what is right, to love mercy, and to walk humbly with your God." While it is true that there was a cry for less social justice issues, I understood that they wanted less black empowerment sermons, which, in my opinion, is a testimony of self-denial and self-hate that has been promoted through Scripture and bought by black Adventists that they must put aside their basic needs for the sake of being unified. It supports what I have been trying to say throughout this document in regards to the injustice that has been done to black Christians through Scripture by divorcing their minds from their bodies. What I mean by this is that their minds are so focused on heavenly things while their bodies are dying policies and structures that are aimed directly at them. Alternatively, their minds are so concerned with focusing on a National Sunday Law and the Pope's whereabouts until they have overlooked the homeless, the sick, the dying, the orphans and the widows on the streets. It is for that reason I realized that I must do more than preaching, in order to convey the truth about social justice found in the Scriptures.

After the untimely deaths of Philando Castile and Alton Sterling it sent America in an uproar and placed blacks and whites on the defense. Some continued the call to fight the power and speak out against injustice done towards blacks. Then there were those that defended the police and said we need to be patient and get all the facts. For the most part, the church was divided. Some as usual decided to ignore it at church but were vocal about it on social media as if to say that discussions like these were only acceptable outside of the church but not inside. This phenomenon was not unique to the members of my context, but to other Seventh-day Adventist members as well. Most of them use social media as an outlet for discussing matters concerning social justice but never fathom or consider doing the same thing at their church. Not much longer after the deaths of Philando Castile and Alton Sterling, a peaceful rally and march that was held in downtown Dallas, turned into mayhem when marksman shot and killed five Dallas police officers.

The news and reactions that was seen on Facebook were alarming. The marches, the protests, the anger, and the distraught were all but too much to process. For that reason, two Wednesday night prayer meeting sessions were dedicated to dealing with the pain. The first Wednesday night session was called "Healing for the Broken." The church was opened with a panel of individuals that were and were not present at the shooting. The panel consisted of four individuals: a bystander, a female, an African-American male, and an army vet. The discussion opened up with prayer and an article written by Cheryl Corley, "Coping While Black: A Season of Traumatic News Takes a Psychological Toll." In that article Cheryl articulately described the trauma and pain that blacks face while living in America. In particular, she highlighted the words Eric Garner said before he took his last breath. "Garner died after an officer put him in a chokehold. "You'll recall that Eric Garner, before he passed, he said, 'I'm tired of you all. I'm tired of you harassing me. I'm tired of you messing with me every day' "; she says, "He was really acknowledging that what he experienced on that one particular day was what he had experienced on many, many other days." Blacks in America carry a heavy load on their shoulders. By continually seeing death after death of people that look like you, it can challenge you psychologically. It will either make you depressed or callous towards the dying.

The session that evening was to basically talk about what was witnessed and how people are coping with it. During the sessions one of the panelists broke down crying when asked if he felt any remorse for the officers. The response of the panelist was a simple, no; "I don't feel sorry for them, because they've been killing us, and no one has any sympathy for us." The statement was followed with tears on behalf of the fear he lives in for his newborn son. Others were emotional as well and just trying to figure out why is all of this happening?

Before we attempted to try to fix the problems, we discovered that we needed to fix us. A trained counselor was also present at the first session to give tips and recommendations of how to deal with trauma and how to channel your anger for positive outcomes and create real change in the lives of individuals. Some of the suggestions were reflecting more on Scripture, praying more than once a day, turning off the television and social media, and spending more time with family and friends.

The second week was about implementation. That session was entitled "I Am Here For You," echoing the words of the little girl in the vehicle when Philando Castile was shot; we wanted to discuss: How can we as a people be there for each other? How can we truly be our brother's keeper and put the neighbor back in the hood? The congregation was ready to participate, and they came with ideas. Some of those ideas were opening up the church for honest dialogue and discussion to encourage members to be able to express themselves without any reservations. The members and visitors that were present committed to being actively present in the community.

A major outcome from the discussions resulted in a voter registration and education day. Upon the realization that in order for real changes to occur, we must attack the polls. By attacking polls means seeking to obtain more positions of power and elect individuals who are genuinely concerned about issues in impoverished communities and the world. It is one thing for a candidate to share the same color as you; but do they share the same values as you? The process that we decided to embark upon was not to simply register people to vote, but to also educate them in regards to what they should look for in a candidate.

Those that volunteered were very dedicated. It was a mixture of all ages, male and female. Every Thursday night leading up to the last day to register individuals to vote, we met at the church to determine ways to be effective in our efforts. The city of Dallas came to deputize the members. Materials were printed, and tshirts were produced. The excitement level of the members to do this was very surprising. This was the first time that the City Temple SDA Church opened its doors for voter registration. Although on the days leading up to the last day to register there was not much traffic, but to see the church move towards this type of action was monumental. It was also very moving to see that it was the members that led the initiative. City Temple was the only church in the Cedar Crest Community that opened their doors for voter registration, and we were the only Seventh-day Adventist church in Dallas to do the same.

One of the volunteers suggested that we visit the local high school in the neighborhood to set up a voter registration booth. Upon talking to the principal and the community liaison, they opened the doors for us to come and register to vote. An entire day was spent at the school encouraging the children to register. Some signed up voluntarily, and to others we had to do a little explaining the power they possessed as voters. I realized that the Latino students were much more willing to sign up; it took a little longer to see some of the African-American students to sign up to vote. Some comments that were made by the African-American students were like, "Why vote, ain't nothing gonna change?" "Voting is stupid." "That's for white people." or the common "I'm good," which simply means leave me alone. The defeat in the speech from our youth is deep rooted. At such a young age they already have the feelings of disenfranchisement and marginalization to feel as if their voices do not-count. I wonder if the same reaction would have been given if these children were attending a school in a better zip code. I could not help but wonder if we would have been met with the same resistance if we were in a white school in the Highland Park area of Dallas, TX. Are African-Americans children discouraged from obtaining positions of power versus white students? Some of the students were confused about voting and did not know how to do it. They asked us questions about who they should vote for. After the day was over, we talked to the community liaison about coming back to school to do some voter education. The liaison informed us that she spoke to the principal about conducting a session on voter education at the school. Unfortunately, the principal informed her that he was not interested in that aspect. You could see the disappointment on the face of the community liaison as well as the volunteers. There was an opportunity to encourage and teach America's future about the power to change the world, and we were stumped with a roadblock on the path to enlightenment. I thought about the endless possibilities and outcomes that could have been brought about if we could have had just one hour to address the students about voting. While I was at the school; I wondered if we could have gone on a tour registering students to vote whilst educating them about the power of vote, their history, and what they can change about the future.

After leaving the school, I felt a bit defeated, but it prompted me to continue to educate and encourage not only myself but also those that are interested in social justice. The week following the voter registration effort, I met with church leaders and we initiated "Temple UniverCity." Temple UniverCity was created as a tool to transform the church to not only a place or worship but also a place of learning. The church must act as not only a place where individuals sing and pray, but it must also be a place of study, reflection, and learning that keeps them relevant to matters concerning their immediate context and the whole world.

I discovered that attendance for our traditional prayer meeting was wavering. City Temple was only averaging about ten to fifteen people per service. However, on the nights when we used the prayer meeting for discussions about the recent shootings, we not only had a great turnout amongst members, but there were a lot of visitors. The discovery showed me that members will travel to talk rather than to have someone talk to them. They will come if a program is planned, presented, and relevant. Temple UniverCity was designed to address that issue. Classes were offered that interested people. We did not cancel the traditional prayer meeting, but instead opened up the other classrooms in the church. There was a total of three classes that were offered for free. We did a grant writing class called "Access Granted," a financial literacy class as well as the "Ubuntu School of Justice."

"Access Granted" was given to teach members in writing grants for public money to fund ministries or programs that would eradicate social justice. Each student was informed that since the class was free, their responsibility was to use the information gathered to write a grant for City Temple SDA. Amazingly, the class was equally divided with participants from City Temple as well as participants from other churches in the Metroplex area. It was the biggest class that was given on Wednesday night.

The financial literacy class was also a big hit amongst the membership. The team that led that initiative targeted two age groups. They sought to teach financial literacy to youth and adults. This class was not given just to teach the children how to be faithful in their tithes and offerings, but instead it was geared to teach the children how to invest and be wise stewards of the money given to them by God. The children learned the true definition of money, and the value of it. Whilst the children learned these tools, the parents were being equipped as well. Parents learned how to put together a budget and manage that budget and how to prioritize for what is important? They learned the differences between needs and wants. Statistically, African Americans live with poor money managing habits and often times do not invest in their future or find ways to leave a legacy.

The mission at City Temple is to establish this new way of thinking in the minds of people to recognize that they should seek to be the lenders and not the borrowers.

The "Ubuntu School of Justice" was introduced as well. After my studies and travels amongst other Seventh-day Adventist congregations social justice has never been a theme or something that was promoted in our churches. My congregation would be concerned and passionate about issues of social justice, but they have never been able to understand the context of the Bible in regards to oppression and domination, and Jesus' work to combat the violence against the marginalized. The Ubuntu School of Justice was created for that purpose: to point the congregation to social justice in the Bible.

The process of naming the school was a battle, and I considered "Charles Dudley School of Justice" because of his passionate work on behalf of black Americans in this country. The Lord led me to the name "Ubuntu," in the tradition of unity and solidarity amongst ourselves. The description of The Ubuntu school of Justice is founded upon the Holy Scriptures and the African tradition of the

Ubuntu. One meaning of "Ubuntu" is correct behavior but correct in this sense is defined by a person's relations with other people. Ubuntu refers to behaving well towards others or acting in ways that benefit the community. Such acts could be as simple as helping a stranger in need or much more complex ways of relating with others. A person who behaves in these ways has 'Ubuntu.' He or she is a full person. One of the most important acts of Ubuntu is understanding and treating one another's needs as holy.

The Scripture admonishes us to allow the same principles to govern our lives. Jesus says, "Do unto others as you have them do unto you." Treat others the same way that you would like to be treated. A major recurring theme is the idea of justice. There are over 100 verses in the Bible that mention the word "justice" or the same theme. Day-to-day we see injustice after injustice. There was a time when the church not only offered spiritual guidance, but it was also the main learning institution in the community. The Ubuntu School of Justice seeks to restore and renew that tradition for our sons, daughters, mothers and fathers. The Ubuntu School of Justice seeks to explore the Scriptures and other writings in a four-week curriculum that looks at various themes of justice in the Word of God. During the four-week-session, students were given reading assignments along with implementation. Students discovered the area of social justice, which God is calling them to apply the concepts and ideas that they have garnered through the various courses.

The four-week sessions did not have as much turn out as the other classes, but there were small groups of six individuals from the church who consistently showed up to do the work and learn. I also opened up the class to the world and live streamed the lessons on Facebook Live. On some evenings we recorded up to 500 viewers with live commentary online. There was a deep interest in matters concerning social justice amongst the SDA church in North America especially amongst Millennials.

Before starting the class, a few surveys were released in the church as well as online. One of the surveys was created for theology majors from our seminary in Berrien Springs, MI as well as Oakwood University which is a HBCU (Historically Black College or University). The questions were:

- What is your definition of social justice?

- During your years at an Adventist school, have you ever had an in-depth study about 'Black Adventist' pioneers?

- Are you aware of the contributions that 'black' Adventists have made in the church and outside of the church?

- Have you been encouraged to read the words of Howard Thurman, Samuel DeWitt Proctor, Frederick Douglas, etc.?

- Have you ever studied any other theologies than Adventist Theology, for example, Black Liberation Theology, Top Down Theology vs. Bottom-Up
Theology, or Jürgen Moltman's Theology of Hope?

- Should Adventists be engaged and vocal on matters concerning social justice?

- Would you like to have a curriculum or track dedicated to biblical social justice?

The answers to the questions were very interesting. In regards to the first question some defined social justice as, 'fighting for the rights and freedoms of all people,' 'advocating for the rights needs of the disempowered of society,' 'ensuring that equity is present in social systems,' and 'granting access to those who are left out.' For the other questions such as: 'During your years at an Adventist school, have you ever had an in-depth study about 'black Adventist pioneers?' All of the participants said no. Some were aware of black Adventists contributions whilst the same group was never encouraged to read the works of Thurman, Proctor, or Douglas. In regards to Adventists being involved in matters concerning social justice, they all agreed that the church should be more vocal on issues of injustice inside and outside of the church. With regards to the question: Would they want to have a curriculum, or a track dedicated to social justice" and the answer was, yes, as well.

The outcome of the survey led me to the conclusion that since social justice is not a theme or a thought in Adventist institutions, some ministers (especially black ones) do not know how to incorporate themes of injustice in their sermons or programs. Therefore, one can surmise that our churches and members do not see social justice as an idea worth exploring. It has also shown that our membership in my context as well as in other contexts do not see black bodies dying, brown bodies being trafficked, mass incarceration, or Palestinian conflict as a part of eschatological teaching.

It is also safe to say that since these theology majors have never had a study on social justice, it would be ludicrous for them to actually encourage their membership to do so or put themes of injustice in their sermons from the text. When I say from the text, I mean seeing the injustice exacted on the Israelites by their oppressors. The same conclusion can be made my context. The previous senior pastors would more than likely answer the questions the same way. If any were to speak on injustice, that would be because of certain things that they have faced personally.

The survey distributed to the members in and outside of the church had some variations in the questions. I wanted to know how old they were to see if social justice was just something that the Millennials were interested in or was it in interest of the older members. Out of 249 responses one participant was under the age of eighteen, and there were two participants over seventy-four years old. The majority of those that filled out the survey were between the ages of twenty-five to forty-four. These are the questions that were asked:

- Can true social justice be accomplished without being politically influenced?

- Should Seventh-day Adventists be involved in politics?

- Does social justice require a lot of money?

- Have you had a Bible study about social justice?

- What is your idea of helping poor people?

- Should justice only be limited to those that are poor?

- Should Seventh-day Adventists be more vocal about the issues minorities face in America?

- Are you a member of City Temple SDA Church?

As far as the first question about being politically influenced was a necessity, the answers were equally split. Some said, yes, they needed to work hand- in- hand with politicians, and others felt that politicians could not be trusted in the fight for justice. I asked this question because for years Adventists have always been apolitical. If the answers were equally split and the majority of the participants were in their mid-twenties to mid-forties, then we can see that there is definitely a shift happening in the church. The body is being more conscious in regards to things that are outside of traditional Seventh-day Adventist last day teachings, or they may be interested in reconciling the fight for justice with their eschatological stance. When asked if Seventh-day Adventists should be more vocal about issues minorities face in America, 91% of the responders said, yes; 2% said, no, and 6% said that they were not sure. Some of the responses to the question were: "SDA's have a responsibility to champion those who are least, lost, and left out," "(Adventists should be) facilitating rallies, peaceful protests, facilitating town hall meetings for the community, being a liaison between the community and law enforcement," "Seventh-day Adventists are apart of the community and are human beings just like other minorities and are affected by injustices like everyone else. Therefore, SDA's should be vocal about issues facing America. Seventh-day Adventists are not (on) an island on its own," and "The head of the church (Ted Wilson) seems to be quite satisfied with the current state of affairs."

The last statement is an indictment on the SDA church. With the recent shootings of unarmed African Americans, it feels as if the church in North America is quite fine as well as the local churches. In these times it is clear that there is a shift in the thinking of the Adventist; more specifically, there appears to be a shift in thinking in regards to young black Adventists and the rest.

Evidently there is a clarion call for SDA's to be more vocal about social issues. Whilst all of this is great, and I am ecstatic about the fact that young Millennial SDA's (as well as other generations) feel compelled to be more actively involved in matters of social justice. When surveying most SDA churches, the ones I have pastored and my current, there are no ministries or departments dedicated to combat social injustice. You will find ministries that are dedicated to charitable acts such as food kitchens, pantries, clothing drives, thanksgiving baskets, etc. The community services department in City Temple is more likened unto community assistance versus community change. I likened the pattern unto misinformed theology majors in regards to having a well-rounded idea of what social justice looks like in the Bible, which leads to misinformed members towards social justice, which is why I decided to start the school of justice at City Temple.

The classes lasted for four weeks. I tried to make the topics as simple as possible but with enough depth that the students would understand social justice as a biblical mandate. The topics were "Charity vs. Change," "Sabbath as Social Justice," "Ellen White and Social Justice," and "Developing a Social Justice Ministry." Numerous announcements were made and the class had six members enrolled, but many other members chose to view the lessons online via Facebook live. I chose to open up the classes online because of the overwhelming responses from the online survey.

A syllabus was distributed and a description of the class equipped with reading materials and objectives for the class. The main objective of the class was to give the members a biblical foundation upon which they would establish their ministry of social justice. The students grasped the understanding that biblical social justice is using the Scriptures to counteract systems that keep people oppressed. We looked at texts such as Amos 5:24, Isaiah 1:17, and Luke 4:18. The Bible is written with the theme of oppression and liberation. Students were then able to identify what the difference between charity and social justice. Charity provides direct services like food, clothing and shelter, whilst justice promotes social change in institutions or political structures. Charity is often times private individual acts, but justice is public, collective actions. Often charity and justice are confused. Members will feel most comfortable and complacent with handing out a few plates of food and jackets. For their homework assignment students were asked to read the article, "The Black Church Dead" by Eddie Glaude, Jr. and then prepare for discussion for the next class. For the most part, the students thoroughly enjoyed the information; the online responses were positive as well.

The second class was entitled "Sabbath as Social Justice." This class was very important in reversing the miseducation of the Seventh-day Adventist. The Sabbath is that one core doctrine that the Adventist church embraces with the belief that this is the line of demarcation, which separates them from other

Christians. Sabbath as social justice sought to define, revisit, and rediscover the true revolutionary and radical teachings of the Sabbath. In Exodus 20:8-11 God gives to Moses the Decalogue or what we know as The Ten Commandments. In the Fourth Commandment God admonishes Israel to "remember the Sabbath day."

The students were taken from the commonly known Exodus commandment to the less popular and overlooked passage in Deuteronomy 5:12-15, wherein God tells the Children of Israel to observe the Sabbath day, but at the end of the passage the text says, "Remember that you were once slaves in Egypt, but the Lord your God brought you out with his strong hand and powerful arm. This is why the Lord your God has commanded you to rest on the Sabbath Day." Students were able to recognize that the Sabbath is tightly linked to social justice because of the Egyptian bondage. The Sabbath becomes an enduring sign of hope that the poor will see justice and the distraught find peace. Through the jubilee year slaves were to be set free, land was to be restored to its original owner, and families were to be reunited.

As the students were enlightened in regards to the establishment of the Sabbath, and that it is often mentioned during moments of oppression. They realized that their Sabbath observance is in direct relation to give liberty and break all oppression. The culminating point of the lesson was displayed when we looked at Jesus' campaign speech in Luke 4:16-18 where he proclaimed that this is the 'acceptable year of the Lord.' The students said that they were especially grateful for the class. They were never taught to see the Sabbath as social justice but rather as an opportunity for them to rest from the worries and cares of the world. During that evening session they were given two articles to read, "Sabbath as Liberation" by Robert B. Kruschwitz, and "God's Economic Justice: Year of Jubilee Deuteronomy 15:1-11" by Reverend William E. Flippin, Jr. Both articles reinforced the concepts given in the class.

The next installment dealt with "Ellen White and Social Justice." Sadly, and unfortunately for many Seventh-day Adventists, when new concepts are ideas are presented to them, it must be validated, backed up and supported by the prophet of the church Ellen G.

White. I knew that this class would be important in laying the foundation for ministries that speak to injustice by showing the students quotes by Ellen G. White that speak on the topic. I pointed the students to a quote found in the book The Southern Work where Ellen White says, "It was never God's purpose that society should be separated into classes, that there should be an alienation between rich and poor, the high and low, the learned and unlearned." In the book Ministry of Healing she admonishes the church that a great work of reform must be done. Reform as defined by the Webster's Dictionary means to change to a better state or form, improve by alteration substitution or abolition. If this is the reform that she is calling for, then it is only right that Adventist seek to make adjustments in a society that attacks the weakest amongst us.

Students were intrigued when they were pointed to the work that Ellen White, her husband James White, and her son Edson White did for the blacks in the southern states. The creation of the 'Gospel Primer' was an evangelistic tool that conveyed messages of the Bible in simple manner that the free slaves could understand. The royalties from the book sales went toward the construction of the Riverboat, called "The Morning Star." Edson White was the point person for the leading work to the blacks in the south. According to Benjamin Baker:

Edson renewed his faith and found a new passion in life when, in 1893 at a Bible study conference in Battle Creek; he came across a tract of his mother's address to the General Conference in 1891 entitled "Our Duty to the Colored People," deciding to engage in educational and evangelistic work for African Americans in the South. After leaguing with another erstwhile Adventist misfit turned good named Will Palmer, the two assembled a group of brave missionaries—many blacks occupying key positions—and called themselves the Southern Missionary Society (SMS). A self-confessed aquamaniac, Edson drafted plans for a riverboat called the Morning Star and had it built at Allegan, Michigan.

The monies collected from the sales of the Gospel Primer coupled with the construction of the Morning Star was used to teach illiterate persons to read. The funds were used to establisha night school, which led to the opening of Oakwood

Industrial School or known today as Oakwood University.

The last installment of the classes was entitled, "Developing a Ministry of Social Justice." Students were walked through the steps of creating a social justice ministry. Although in the first class we defined social justice, students were taught the components of a social justice ministry. It is a ministry that not only ministers to the person but also addresses systems that create the individual's needs. The only way that this goal could be accomplished, I told the students that they had to discover what their passion was. What is it that disturbs them or bothers them constantly? They were told that their passion was whatever breaks their hearts. If it is a passion, then the individual would be more apt to do it rather than to see it as something they were given or simply a job. If it breaks your heart, then you are more likely to work towards implementing change. After they have discovered what breaks their hearts, they were told to pray about it. I have personally discovered that when I pray about what breaks my heart, God opens doors and leads me to individuals who share the same passion. God also puts people in your circle that share the same passion as you. After the students were told to pray about whatever breaks their hearts, I encouraged them to become experts at their topic, to know it well, to read every article, book, and to attend seminars about the issue. When they become experts at it, they will begin to speak about it, and folks will hear them and begin to use them as a point of reference. The students were encouraged to start developing relationships with entities outside of the church. One of the things that damage our church is the fact that we do not seek ways to work with others and build healthy, long- lasting relationships, which is comparable to separatist theology. For the ministry to take off, Adventists must embrace the fact that they may not be the only ones in the struggle for liberation. There are others that we can learn from. Last, but definitely not least, the class was informed on how to create their mission and vision statement. The mission statement is the purpose of this ministry, and the vision statement is how do you imagine this ministry taking off and its results.

When I asked the students what things that break their hearts, they told me that they were hurt by the way orphans were treated. Another student told me that she was heartbroken about the food deserts in our community. She said that since she is a Seventh Day Adventists and we profess to have a message of health and restoration, it is disheartening to know that we exist and are comfortable with the proliferation of greasy foods and liquor stores in impoverished communities.

I was particularly intrigued with the work of one of my students. This particular individual wanted to address the issue of poor health care services in impoverished communities. In her document, she explained that, the experience of many African American families is that certain hospitals, who historically have not served African Americans or persons who receive Medicare or Medicaid are disparately victimized with a lack of correct diagnosis and quality medical treatment, which can lead to premature death or family being pressured to make decisions about something that they are not well informed about. The desire to do this grew out of their own experience with hospitals and losing family members. Some of the solutions offered are to have a "Senior Citizens Health Fair" to offer advice to the elderly and to those that care for them.

Another student expressed that they would like to see programs implemented to educate the underskilled so that they would have a better sense of accomplishment. The student's desire is to furnish second- hand stores with professional attire so that those who are looking for employment can be dressed successfully for their interview and supplying temporary homesteads for families with a game plan for permanent housing. They would also like to implement a program for businesses to build restaurants for the homeless to eat a variety of items on the menu to their self-worth.

Some students did not or could not tell me right there, but I could see that they were thinking and processing what they wanted to create. Overall, the reviews of the classes were all positive. The students were happy and pleased with all the information provided to them.

I personally was hoping that more members would have been willing to attend the classes, but I understand that there are always challenges in the personal lives of the laity. I had lofty dreams that the class on social justice would have been bursting at the seams since I had made so many strides in regards with presenting sermons from a contemporary social justice angle. I did learn something throughout the process, and it was a valuable lesson. The lesson that I learned was that you cannot base success on numbers. Large crowds do not necessarily equate with success. I have learned to be content with accomplishments. What transpired at City Temple SDA Church has never been done to the level that was brought in the last three years. Never had the church done a voter registration drive. They never joined forces with another congregation outside of their denomination to have a national action night. As a church body, we gathered to watch and discuss Ava Duvenray's riveting documentary called "Thirteenth" and have a discussion.

This process has pushed me to recreate and rewrite the mission statement for City Temple. The mission statement is rooted in Jesus' message in the temple found in Luke 4:16-18. It says, "Our mission is to follow the example of Jesus by bringing news of victory to the poor, comfort the brokenhearted, release the prisoner, give sight to the blind, and set the oppressed free." We acknowledge that our church stretches beyond the four walls, and the community is our congregation. The vision statement says, "Our vision is that the City Temple Seventh-day Adventist Church would be a place that all people can feel like they are home. We are to share the love and gospel of Jesus Christ to build stronger families, stronger communities, and stronger disciples that transform our world." It was my desire to give the church an identity. Other churches are known for their singing; some are known for their work with families, but our church should be known for its prophetic engagement and social justice. When people come to City Temple then they should know what we stand for and our purpose. I am sure that I will lose a lot of members because there are many who feel that this mission and vision are not in line with traditional SDA teachings, but you have got to lose some things before you can gain new things.

The mission and vision statement led me to also create the Bill of Rights for the Underserved. Jeremiah
29:7 says, "And work for the peace and prosperity of the city where I sent you into exile. Pray to the

Lord for it, for it's welfare will determine your welfare." Since the mission of our church stretches beyond the four walls, we seek the shalom of the city. This is visualized by cleaning the street, planting trees, feeding the poor, shutting down immoral businesses, and embracing people from every ethnic background. For that reason, the Bill of Rights states:

- Equality: We believe that people care created equally by one God. Yet there are those that have been pushed to the margins of society and treated less than a human being. We see this as much more than a civil right, but as a basic human right to be treated equally.

- Freedom: We seek physical and spiritual freedom from anything anyone, or any system that continues to push a marginalized people further away.

- Economic Justice: We seek for a fair distribution of wealth amongst all people. All people should have access to the earth's natural resources.

- Environment Justice: We seek a proper management of God's earth, especially with those in impoverished neighborhoods. We seek to end illegal dumping that tarnishes and destroys communities of black and brown people.

- Quality Housing: We seek housing for all individuals regardless of income. Today in Texas there are many who live without basic necessities. We seek to end slumlords who intentionally exploit the poor.

- Prison Reform: We seek to end the warehousing of black and brown bodies. We seek that all prisoners receive fair treatment medically and mentally.

Right now, it appears to be a tall glass to drink, but it is a start. It is a journey on a road with a lot of twists and turns, but a road that I am willing to travel, and I am glad that I have a few members who want to accompany me. Doing this work has driven me a lot, and it continues to push me. It has driven me to discover a lot more about myself and to recreate myself to be the person that I strongly believe God is calling me to be. The tenure of a Seventh-day Adventist pastor in a church on average is between four to seven years.

My calling is to make the church better, and stronger for the next pastor who will occupy the seat of administration. My predecessor Eddie

Polite did exactly that. He labored and toiled for seven years at City Temple. When I asked him why he decided to take a bold leap and create the "Live Well Center," he said, "In the book, Ministry of Healing, by Ellen G. White, we stumbled upon this thought: "Christ's method alone will give true success in reaching the people. The Savior mingled with men as one who desired their good. He showed His sympathy for them, ministered to their needs, and won their confidence. Then He bade them, "Follow Me." Remodeling our ministry after Christ's ministry in order to realize "true" success became our magnificent obsession! It also gave birth to a vision of establishing an outreach center within our community that could meet the needs of the underserved on a regular basis rather than making cameo appearances in the community on an annual basis. Establishing this center would also afford us the opportunity to establish community relationships, relevance, and trust—a valuable commodity for building community influence. These words are so valuable. This was the beginning of the shift in the church and leadership. My desire and passion was to use this foundation as a platform to build upon and create more opportunities to help the least of these.

We are in a pivotal moment in black America's history and the black church. We have just elected to the highest office in our nation who has no political background or experience. An individual whose claim to fame was about questioning the birth of Barak Obama, an individual who used racist rhetoric, and bullying to climb to the top. Those that have been summoned to provide protection have been shooting us, and their defense is "I feared for my life." The church has been dormant and dead, and now it is time for us to embody the character and actions of Nehemiah by going back to our communities and rebuilding the walls. It is time for us to embody the words and actions of Jesus Christ who went back to Nazareth, as His custom was and stood up in the temple and declared that He has come to bring good news to the poor, heal the brokenhearted, set the captives free, give sight to the blind, and set at liberty those that have been bruised. It is the fierce urgency of now, and for that reason we cannot afford to be silent.

I do realize that there is a strong possibility that I will get transferred to another church in maybe another state or region; it has always been my desire to leave whatever church I occupy in a better place that I found it. Hopefully the following pastor does not have to work too hard, but he can always build upon it. Then there is always the possibility that some pastor will come behind me and destroy everything that was implemented at City Temple. I am optimistic that throughout my tenure that there will be more buy in, and if there is not, then I will still be content. A colleague in ministry once told me that not everyone will catch your vision. There are always three types of people in every church: the 'thirties', the 'sixties' and the 'nineties.' If you give them a seed from an apple tree, ninety percent will only see an apple tree coming from that seed, sixty percent will see an orchard, but the thirty percent will see the tree, the orchard, apple juice, apple cider, apple pie, apple turnovers, and endless apple opportunities. For anyone that will read this, stay encouraged and follow the path that God has set for you. Hopefully, the membership at City Temple SDA will be so strong that they will not divert from the mission and the call to help the helpless, defend the defenseless, and be a voice for the voiceless as we wait for the soon and imminent return of our Lord and Savior Jesus Christ.

WHAT SHOULD YOU DO?

13

I need to start this chapter off by informing you that the work of social justice can be long, slow, and arduous. That's what makes it different from charity or charitable acts. Social justice wins don't come overnight. In some cases, it may not even come in your lifetime. If you were to take a case study of some of the greatest civil rights leaders known throughout history, most of them never lived long enough to see the impact of the work that they have done on behalf of the least of these. It's because of that reason, most people would opt to do charitable work, and be comfortable with charitable acts because the results are immediate. Feeding and clothing the homeless will provide for us temporal and immediate fix whilst not addressing the systemic problem in our society. As stated before, the work of social justice is to eliminate the need for charitable acts. We are working for basic human rights for all people. You and I understand that our faith doesn't push us to do this great work, but we are pulled by the Spirit to move and act because we love God's creation and believe in equality.

What are the steps towards creating a viable and sustainable social justice ministry for my congregation? Whether you are full-time or a bi-vocational minister, please know that you cannot do this work by yourself, you need a team. Often times are tempted to do everything on our own. The biggest problem with doing it on our own is that we are humans. We have limitations. We have setbacks and hectic lives. Social justice is so broad and so deep that it is impossible to work and fight on behalf of others by yourself effectively. The acts of injustice are so prevalent and frequent that it makes it so hard to breathe. Every time you pick your head up to catch a breath, there is another senseless act of injustice. When you become overwhelmed with not only managing and leading a congregation, but to add social justice work to it, it can make you want to throw in the towel and give up. Let me say this one more time, you need a team!

THE BLUEPRINT

In the previous chapter we looked at Nehemiah, and our discovery was that although he did not live in Jerusalem at the time of the burning down of the walls, he was still concerned and motivated to restore infrastructure and stability to his community. Nehemiah did what I believe all of us need to practice. He was informed; he prayed; he used his allies; he organized, and then he restores infrastructure for the community. We will refer to this as "The Nehemiah Project."

When you are attempting to do the work of community revitalization and advocacy, it is all important that you are informed in regards to the prevalent issues. As members of the body of Christ we often times think that we know everything, and with boldness we believe that we are qualified to speak on the matter at hand. One of the biggest problems with social media is that it gives any and every one the platform to talk about things that they have no idea about. It makes everyone an expert with great advice. In reality, if we take things for what they are, the church can oftentimes be a place full of experts. They are experts at telling you how to live your life. Often times it's that same attitude that we use towards the community that we are serving. We organize ourselves in the church with a 'know it all, how to fix the community mentality" that only shows how misinformed about the real problem that is at hand.

I will never forget one of my first experiences with being confronted with the truth. My church is located in a community with the usual suspects, processed food, liquor stores, cash payday loan shops, car title loan shops, and a local drop out factory called a high school with its feeder, the elementary school. On a few occasions I was blessed to attend a few community meetings held at the school. One evening I had a great conversation with the community liaison. She told me about the alarming number of students that were failing their classes, and I was so discouraged and defeated. These were kids' ages ranged from 8-12. Upon receiving that information, I organized a team at the church, and we were sure that we had the answer. We knew that the reason why the kids were failing their classes was because they had bad teachers. Failing students is a result of failing teachers. Obviously, that was the answer. So, we formulated a plan to advocate for better teachers. I took time to sit down with my leaders who were interested in addressing the problem. We formulated the plan to advocate for better teachers. The task was upon us to remove the unworthy teachers who were just there to collect a paycheck with teachers who cared about the students that they were serving.

We scheduled another meeting with the school community liaison as well as the principal. Some teachers from the school were in attendance as well. We began digging deeper into the issues when it came to the students. During our discussion one of my leaders said, "We would like to advocate for better and more teachers." Suddenly silence encompassed the entire room, and it was at the moment we gave a reality check. The principal informed us that she had some of the best teachers that our state had to offer. She took her time when building her team because she cared about the students that were under her care. Then the hammer dropped. She told us that we didn't need better teachers or better facilities and that these kids needed breakfast, attention, and some good 'ol tender love and care. She informed us that our teachers didn't have the time to teach the curriculums that they had prepared, because the beginning part of the school day involved having them to brush their teeth, comb their hair, and, at times, taking a rag to wipe them up. The children came to school with a bag of chips and soda (pop) in their hands. In some cases, they needed to sleep because they went to bed so late.

I was embarrassed because I did what I believed so many of us do: We use our privilege to assume that we know what people need. I would argue that it was a Christian thing! You know, people need Jesus first, before they get the hot meal. Our brains are warped in some way to think that a hungry person would be receptive to reading a book about salvation before they eat. Our energy and efforts went into figuring out how we could advocate for better teachers when all we needed to do was figure out how we could start a food program for the children, or, even better, support the food program that was already in place. (Please pay attention to this point): you don't have to reinvent the wheel. Social justice does not always require us to create something new, but it can also mean that we find ways to support systems that are already established.

Now, I am not saying that there is anything wrong with setting an agenda, but the number one item on the schedule should be discovering the problem. There's no better way to do that than to go to the problem or bring the issue to you. Setting the agenda for your community can have adverse outcomes, thus resulting in positive energy going towards something that never had any legs. When that happens, you end up dealing with burnout and feelings of letting go and reverting to what you knew before, because you did not see the results that you were hoping for. Stick with this book because I'm going to talk a little bit about burnout later on.

PRAYER

When you are informed about the issues before you, then you know what to pray about. The advancement of social justice work in your community will not work unless the Lord is in it and in you. The Scriptures are writing within the context of oppression and liberation. God advocates for the poor extensively in the sacred texts. If you need direction in that area, then I would strongly recommend picking up the 'Poverty and Social Justice' Bible. It has every reference and story that relates to social justice highlighted for further and more in-depth study.

If you are reading this book, then you already know about the importance of prayer. You are acutely aware of the fact that prayer can move mountains and open doors.

You know that God loves it when we pray, but God also loves it when we know what to ask for. The God that you and I serve hates injustice. Proverbs 17:15 says, "Acquitting the guilty and condemning the innocent, both are detestable to the Lord" (NLT). In Deuteronomy 25:13-16 God says, "You must use accurate scales when you weigh out merchandise, and you must use full and honest measures. Yes, always use honest weights and measures, so that you may enjoy a long life in the land the Lord your God is giving you. All who cheat with dishonest weights and measures are detestable to the Lord your God" (NLT). God does not favor those who unfairly distribute resources. Economic distribution is important to God. When the powerful or even God's children use their energy to exploit the weak and vulnerable, God is not moved. Let me repeat myself. God hates injustice. Therefore, it is only right that God's children pray for strength to combat prejudice. Not only does God detest injustice, but I am sure that He will give you the tools that you need to fight against it.

When I began to love justice and mercy, I did not know where to start. I admired so many people who were doing it, but I had no clue in regards to how they got there. I started praying for the things that I cared about the most. Andy Stanley says, "The way to discover your passion is to look at what breaks your heart." Injustice broke my heart, and inequality is intolerable to me. I am so heartbroken by injustice, and I vividly remember crying after watching certain episodes of law and order. Just the other day I cried while I was watching "Dear White People," particularly the episode when the campus police pulled out guns on Reggie, and I cried like a baby when I watched "Crash" and "Fruit vale Station." I knew what I wanted to pray about. When I asked the Lord to show me the way to advocate for social justice, He opened up the floodgates. God has a beautiful way or leading you to the right people and leading the right people to you.

There have been so many instances when God has just brought individuals into my circle who share the same passion as I do. By bringing those people to me, they have led me to other circles that have led to my development and pursuit of justice. I have to insert this warning right here: When you start praying about your passion, you will get an answer to your prayer; the results can be overwhelming. You will begin to meet so many people and be asked to do so many things that you may not even have enough time to complete them all. I guess this is a significant problem. It's great to see how God can take what seemed like a daunting mountain and level it for you so that you can have clarity and clear vision.

I am clearly assuming that if you are praying about a particular issue, then you are serious about it. As you pray about it, you should also read about the issue that you want to deal with. Become an expert at it so that when you speak on the topic, you communicate the problems brilliantly. Become the resident pro on that particular thing. The people that the Lord will lead to you will not only be attracted to your spiritual connection to God but also to the way you speak so passionately and eloquently about social justice. You will have learners and contributors around, who want to see God's will manifest itself in this world.

BUILDING YOUR TEAM

You can definitely do social justice work by yourself, but you will be more effective with a team. You will need a group of people that share the same passion as you. More than likely this will be from the same group of people that you have prayed for and the woman the Lord sent to you. I encourage everyone that I meet that you want to keep this group small and strategic. To begin, you don't need more than five to seven people. When too many people are in a room, you will have to spend so much time filtering opinions, and decisions will never get made. I always land on the number of five to seven people because the reality is that in most cases you probably will not get more than five to seven people to commit to social justice. Social justice work is not easy. It's not as popular as marching or showing up at the food kitchen. Social justice is thankless and behind the scenes. Folks will always show up for the events, which is excellent. Numbers are always needed at public demonstrations; they show solidarity and collective reasoning on the matter at hand. Your justice team will be the one thinking and processing how to keep the main thing the main thing.

If you are a pastor reading this, please keep in mind that your justice team is not your charity team, which means that they will not be planning opportunities to do health fairs. Instead, they will be looking at how we can ensure that sick people can get their medication or advocate for ways to bring fresh produce to the neighborhood.

Be very strategic when formulating your justice team. At least one of those individuals should be able to attend community meetings. They should be able to run and oversee your justice team. As a pastor you are way too busy to do it, and even as a lay person, you are way too busy to do this by yourself. Remember: You do not have to do everything. I am sure that there is probably a well-respected community activist group in your neighborhood that would love to partner with you. Faith in Texas sends a representative to my church to help my justice team organize for action. Ideally, as a pastor you want your justice team to be able to stand on their own two feet. When your justice team is moving and operating at an optimal level, you should be able to stay abreast of their movements. Regular meetings with your lead organizer are pivotal. As the pastor or lay leader, you always want to know what is going on so that surprise never catches you. To get your team operating like a well-oiled machine will take some time, but it can get there. It's going to require some hands-on work from you, but pace yourself and be very patient. Your team must be comprised of individuals who are self-motivated and have the heart for redeeming people. This is why the teaching and preaching series is critical! The individuals that come out of that training will be the ones who will carry your church into uncharted territories.

THE SLOW AND THE SERIOUS

14

I know that I keep saying this, but the work of social justice is a slow turning wheel. Victories do not come overnight in most cases. It requires much dedication and time; that is why some people do it as a full-time job. There are courses and degrees offered by so many institutions that focus on social justice. Individuals are continually studying and gathering statistics on the topic of social justice and its many tentacles.

One of the things that make social justice so tricky is that the moment you focus on one thing, something else pops up. For example, when Trayvon Martin died, and the verdict was released, we had to deal with the death of Michael Brown. Then there was Philando Castille, Alton Sterling, Walter Scott, Sandra Bland only to name a few. Please keep in mind I'm just talking about unarmed black men who have been shot. In the era of

Trumpism we witnessed the ban on individuals coming to America from certain countries, the deportation of our Latin brothers and sisters, and the Dakota Pipeline crisis that is affecting so many Native

Americans. Earth justice was threatened when the President referred to Global warming as something made up by the Chinese. When it comes to the earth's population or merely just the earth, there has been an attack. This book is not even giving us a worldview outlook to violations of human rights. Just reading this paragraph can give you a migraine because I have not even scratched the surface; I'm confident that you could come up with so many other atrocities occurring against God's creation.

You need to pace yourself! Tackle one thing at a time. You will not win every battle when it comes to social justice, and to be honest, you may not even see it in your lifetime. That was something challenging for me to accept. When I first started the work, I wanted to see the change immediately. The Lord sat me down and told me to look at most of my heroes from Isaiah, Micah, Hosea, and Amos. (I could go on for chapters); all of them were persecuted for what they stood for. Then I looked at my modern-day heroes: Martin Luther King Jr., Steven Biko, Marcus Garvey, Malcolm X, Fred Hampton, and Huey P. Newton (I could go on for chapters), and all died before they saw the change they were fighting for. I am not saying that has to be you, but it's a reality in regards to how serious this work is. Learn to be okay with some losses. Always remember that not everything you lose is a loss. Sometimes you have to lose to gain something new. There have been times when I have walked away so defeated because a plan didn't work out, or a bill did not get passed. Defeat can make you want to give up. Use every stone that life throws at you or every failure as the opportunity to regroup and come back stronger.

CELEBRATE

We spent a little time talking about defeat, but I want to talk to you about victories. Although you will have some disappointments, you are going to have some wins; and when you do have those, celebrate the moment. Enjoy it because there is so much work to do; we hardly take the time to say, "God did this through me!" Often, we do not do it because we do not view it as something major, or we are too busy thinking about what is our next move. Stop! Take your team out to dinner and debrief about the challenges and the experience. What did you learn about this, and how can we use this as a stepping stone for our next action? Constantly in the Scriptures we would read over and over about those moments when Jesus would talk to the disciples about what they just witnessed or why they could not do a particular task. Taking time to pause is all about the growth and development that you and your team desperately need.

Just remember that what you did, could have been done through anyone else, but God decided to use you because your heart was in the right place. So, whether that was going down to the state capital to talk to a state representative about a bill that needs to be passed, standing with some immigrants in front of a detention center, or showing up in court for a juvenile that is being tried as an adult, that is major, and you deserve a party. Trust me, you will appreciate it, and your team will enjoy I, too. Everybody needs affirmation, and there can never be too much of it going around. Validation is essential in the work of social justice. People join gangs for validation. All of these reality shows and the search for the next celebrity are a part of our human quest for acceptance and validation. If it is so important to us in our daily activities, then why can't it be the same for us in our spiritual, social justice efforts?

Last but not least, thank God for you. Thank God that you were created and made for this. I remember when I bought my first car, it was a black 2008 BMW 550i. It was a beautiful piece of metal. I took it to my mechanic one day because I wanted to have a module put inside of the car to integrate the iPhone capabilities. When I took it to the mechanic, he informed me that there was nothing that I had to do. He said that everything that you need is inside of the car already; all I had to do was open up the center console, and the connections were in there. I was embarrassed and blessed at the same time. I was ashamed because I felt like I should've known this already and blessed because I saved a whole lot of money, but the words that stood out to me was "Everything I needed was already there." I shared that story with you because everything you need, God has already put inside of you. You need to open up the center of your heart and discover the module and let God plug His heart inside of yours!

Resist. Redeem. Reclaim. Renew!

BIBLIOGRAPHY

Achtemeier, P. J. Harper's Bible Dictionary. San Francisco, CA: Harper and Row; Society of Biblical Literature, 1985.

Adeny, Walter F., and Walter Frederic. Expositor's Bible: Ezra, Nehemiah, and Esther. New York, NY: Funk and Wagnalls Company, 2012. Kindle.

Allen, Ronald J., Dale P. Andrews, and Dawn Ottoni-Wilhelm. Preaching God's Transforming Justice: A Lectionary Commentary, Year A.

Louisville, KY: Westminster John Knox Press, 2011. _____. Preaching God's Transforming Justice: A Lectionary Commentary, Year B.

Louisville, KY: Westminster John Knox Press, 2011. _____. Preaching God's Transforming Justice: A Lectionary Commentary, Year C.

Louisville, KY: Westminster John Knox Press, 2011. Anderson, Claud. Black Labor, White Wealth: The Search for Power and Economic Justice. Bethesda, MD: PowerNomics Corporation of America, 1994.

Asante, Molefi Kete. Afrocentricity: The Theory of Social Change. Chicago, IL: African American Images, 2003.

Ayers, Danielle L., and Reginald W. Williams Jr. To Serve This Present Age: Social Justice Ministries in the Black Church. Valley Forge, PA: Judson Press, 2013. Kindle.

Baker, Benjamin. "Adventism's Aquamaniac." Blacksdahistory.org. June 2011. Accessed January 1, 2017. http://www.blacksdahistory.org/Adventism_s_Una ppreciated_Aquamaniac.html.

Barry, J. D., M. S. Heise, M. Custis, D. Mangum, and M. M. Whitehead. Faithlife Study Bible. Bellingham, WA: Lexham Press, 2012.

Beito, David T., and Linda Royster Beito. Black Maverick: T. R. M. Howard's Fight for Civil Rights and Economic Power. Champaign, IL: University of Illinois Press, 2009. Accessed August 1, 2014. http://www.blackpast.org/aah/howard-t-rm-1908-1976#sthash.XQ4uBJxS.dpuf.

Birch, Bruce C. Let Justice Roll Down: The Old Testament, Justice, and Christian Life. Louisville, KY: Westminster John Knox, 1991.

Blount, B. K., C. H. Felder, C. J. Martin, and E. B. Powery. True to Our Native Land: An African American New Testament Commentary. Minneapolis, MN: Fortress Press, 2007.

Bock, Darrel L. The IVP New Testament Commentary Series: Luke. Downers Grove, IL: InterVarsity Press, 1994.

Boone, Linwood. The Effects of Internal Oppression on Educated African Americans in the Worship Experience. Dayton, OH: United Theological Seminary, 2001.

Brueggemann, Walter. Prophetic Imagination: Revised Edition. Minneapolis, MN: Fortress Press, 2001. Kindle.

_____. Sabbath as Resistance. Louisville, KY: Westminster John Knox Press, 2014. Kindle.

Bryson, Theodore H. Getting Beyond the Four Walls. Dayton, OH: United Theological Seminary, 2003.

Campbell, Steve. "A Growing Divide Between Rich and Poor in Texas." Star-Telegram. January 28, 2014. Accessed January 28, 2014. http://www.startelegram.com/2014/01/28/5521495/a-growingdivide-between-rich.html#storylink=cpy.

Carter, Warren. Matthew and the Margins: A Political and Religious Reading. Maryknoll, NY: Orbis Books, 2000.

Cassidy, Richard. Jesus, Politics, and Society: A Study on the Book of Luke. Eugene, OR: Wipf and Stock Publishers, 1978.

Chappell, David L. A Stone of Hope: Prophetic Religion and the Death of Jim Crow. Chapel Hill, NC; London, UK: The University of North Carolina Press, 2004.

City Temple SDA Church. "Dallas City Temple 90th Anniversary Celebration Journal." Personal newsletter, October 1, 2005.

Cone, James. A Black Theology of Liberation. Maryknoll, NY: Orbis Books, 1945.

_____. The Cross and the Lynching Tree. Maryknoll, NY: Orbis Books, 2011.

Corbett, Steve, and Brian Fikkert. When Helping Hurts: How to Alleviate Poverty Without Hurting the Poor . . . and Yourself. Chicago, IL: Moody Publishers, 2014. Kindle. Corley, Cheryl. "Coping While Black: A Season of Traumatic News Takes a Psychological Toll." NPR. July 2, 2015. Accessed January 1, 2017. http://www.npr.org/sections/codeswitch/2015/07/0 2/419462959/coping-while-black-a-season-oftraumatic-news-takes-a-psychological-toll.

Cowen, Tyler. "The United States of Texas: Why the Lone State is America's Future." Time Magazine 182, no. 18 (October 28, 2013): 2.

Day, Keri. Unfinished Business: Black Women, the Black Church, and the Struggle to Thrive in America. Maryknoll, NY: Orbis Books,

2012. Kindle. DeYoung, Curtiss Paul, and Allan Aubrey Boesak. Radical Reconciliation: Beyond Political Pietism and Christian Quietism. Maryknoll, NY: Orbis Books, 2012. Kindle.

Dorrien, Gary. The New Abolition: W. E. B. Dubois and the Black Social Gospel. New Haven, CT: Yale University Press, 2015.

Dybdahl, Jon L. Andrews Study Bible. Berrien Spring, MI: Andrews University Press, 2010. Enns, P. P. The Moody Handbook of Theology. Chicago, IL: Moody Press, 1989.

Evans, J. H., Jr. We Have Been Believers: An African American Systematic Theology. Minneapolis, MN: Fortress Press, 2012.

Fisher, Holly. "Oakwood College Students' Quest for Social Justice Before and During the Civil Rights Era." The Journal of African American History 88, no. 2 (Spring 2003): 110-125. Flippin, William E., Jr. "God's Economic Justice: Year of Jubilee Deuteronomy 15:1-11." Huffington Post. Updated January 13, 2012. Accessed March 23, 2014. http://www.huffingtonpost.com/reverend-williame-flippin-jr/jubilee_b_1195232.html.

Food Empowerment Project. "Food Deserts." Foodispower.org. Accessed February 4, 2014. http://www.foodispower.org/food-deserts/.

Francis, Leah Gunning. Ferguson and Faith: Sparking Leadership and Awakening Community. St. Louis, MO: Chalice Press, 2015. Kindle.

Franklin, Robert M. Crisis in the Village: Restoring Hope in African American Communities. Minneapolis, MN: Fortress Press, 2007. Kindle.

Freeman, Lance. There Goes the Hood: Views of Gentrification from the Ground Up. Philadelphia, PA: Temple University Press, 2006. Kindle.

Glaude, Eddie S., Jr. "The Black Church is Dead." Huffington Post. Updated August 23, 2012. Accessed August 28, 2013. http://www.huffingtonpost.com/eddie-glaude-jrphd/the-black-church-is-dead_b_473815.html.

_____. Democracy in Black: How Race Still Enslaves the American Soul. New York, NY: Crown Publishing, 2016.

Goetz, Edward G. New Deal Ruins: Race, Economic Justice, and Public Housing Policy. Ithaca, NY: Cornell University Press, 2013. Kindle.

Gordon, Brubacher. Principles of Jubilee in the Old Testament, and for the Enduring Community of Faith: Holy Land Hollow Jubilee.

London, UK: Melisende, 1999. Gutiérrez, Gustavo. A Theology of Liberation. Maryknoll, NY: Orbis Books, 1988.

Gutiérrez, Gustavo, and Gerhard Ludwig Müller. On the Side of the Poor: The Theology of Liberation. Maryknoll, NY: Orbis Books, 2015.

Harris, Forrest E. Ministry for Social Crisis, Theology and Praxis in the Black Church Tradition.

Macon, GA: Mercer University Press, 1993.

Harris, Frederick C. Something Within: Religion in African American Political Activism. Oxford, UK: Oxford University Press, 1999.

Harvey, Robert S. "Restoring the Social Justice Identity of the Black Church." Inquiries Journal. 2010. Accessed November 18, 2014. http://www.inquiriesjournal.com/articles/162/resto ring-the-social-justice-identity-of-the-black-church. Hendricks, Obery. The Politics of Jesus:

Rediscovering the True Revolutionary Nature of the Teachings of Jesus and How They Have Been Corrupted. New York, NY: Double Day, 2006.

_____. The Universe Bends Toward Justice: Radical Reflections on the Bible, the Church, and the Body Politic. Maryknoll, NY: Orbis Books, 2011. Hendrikson, William. New Testament

Commentary: Exposition of the Gospel of Luke. Grand Rapids, MI: Baker Book House, 1996.

Henriques, Hilari. The Everlasting Gospel Versus the Social Gospel. Accessed April 2, 2015. http://prophesyagain.org/the-everlasting-gospelvs-the-social-gospel/#more-659.

Hill, Marc Lamont. Nobody: Casualties of America's War on the Vulnerable, from Ferguson to Flint and Beyond. New York, NY: Simon and Schuster, 2016.

Jacobsen, Dennis A. Doing Justice: Congregations and Community Organizing. Minneapolis, MN: National Book Network, 2001. Kindle.

Jamieson, R., A. R. Fausset, and D. Brown. Commentary Critical and Explanatory on the Whole Bible. Vol. 2. Oak Harbor, WA: Logos Research Systems, 1997.

Jones, Damon R. Teaching for Prophetic Social Action: Empowering Christian Educators to Transform Students. Trotwood, OH: United Theological Seminary, 2008.

Keener, Craig S. The IVP Bible Background Commentary. Downers Gove, IL: Intervarsity Press, 2014.

Kinsler, Ross, and Gloria Kinsler. The Biblical Jubilee and the Struggle for Life: An

Invitation to Personal, Ecclesial, and Social Transformation. Maryknoll, NY: Orbis Books, 2000.

Knight, George R. A Brief History of Seventhday Adventists. Hagerstown, MD: Review and Herald Publishing Association, 2013. Kindle. Kruschwitz, Robert B. "Sabbath as Liberation." Christian Reflection. Center for Christian Ethics. 2012. Accessed May 18, 2015. http://www.baylor.edu/ifl/christianreflection/Sabbathstudyguide1.pdf.

Linthicum, Robert. Transforming Power: Biblical Strategies for Making a Difference in Your Community. Downers Grove, IL: Intervarsity Press, 2003.

_____. Building a People of Power, Equipping Churches to Transform their Communities. Colorado Springs, CO: Authentic Publishing, 2006.

London, Samuel G., Jr. Seventh-day Adventists and the Civil Rights Movement. Jackson, MS: University Press of Mississippi, 2009. Kindle.

_____. "The Sociopolitical Activism of Warren S. Banfield." Paper presented at the MPSA Annual National Conference, Palmer House Hilton Hotel, Chicago, IL, April 3, 2008. Lopez, Ian Haney. Dog Whistle Politics: How Coded

Racial Appeals Have Reinvented Racism and Wrecked the Middle Class. New York, NY: Oxford University Press, 2013. Kindle. Louw, J. P., and E. A. Nida. Greek-English

Lexicon of the New Testament: Based on Semantic Domains. Vol. 1. New York, NY: United Bible Societies, 1996.

Marshall, Howard I. The New International Greek Testament Commentary: The Gospel of Luke. Grand Rapids, MI: The Paternoster Press, 1978. Maxwell, David. Race in a Post-Obama America: The Church Responds. Louisville, KY: Westminster John Knox Press, 2016.

McCorn, Lester Agyei. Standing on Holy Common Ground. Chicago, IL: MMGI Books, 2013.

McKinney, Lora Ellen. Christian Education in the African American Church. Valley Forge, PA: Judson Press, 2003.

McMickle, Marvin. Where Have All the Prophets Gone? Reclaiming Prophetic Preaching in America. Cleveland, OH: Pilgrim Press, 2006. Milgorm, Jacob. Jubilee: A Rallying Cry for Today's Oppressed, Holy Land Hollow Jubilee: God, Justice and the Palestinians. London, UK:

Melisende, 1999. Moltmann, Jürgen. "Liberating and Anticipating the Future." In Liberating Eschatology:

Essays in Honor of Letty M. Russell. Edited by Margaret A. Farley and Serene Jones. Louisville, KY: Westminster John Knox Press, 1999.

_____. Theology of Hope: On the Grounds and the Implications of a Christian Eschatology. Minneapolis, MN: Fortress Press, 1993.

Morgan, Campbell G. Pulpit Legends: A Bible Survey from Genesis to Revelation. Chattanooga, TN: AMG Publishers, 1993.

Morgan, Douglas. The Peacemaking Remnant: Essays and Historical Documents. Kearney, NE: Morris Publishing, 2005.

Mullane, Deirdre, ed. Crossing the Dangerous Waters: Three Hundred Years of African-American Writing: The Talented Tenth by W. E. B. Dubois. New York, NY: Anchor Books, 1993.

Myers, Ched, Marie Dennis, Joseph Nangle, Cynthia Moe-Lobeda, and Stuart Taylor. Say to This Mountain: Mark's Story of Discipleship. Maryknoll, NY: Orbis Books, 1996.

Page, Hugh R. The Africana Bible: Reading Israel's Scriptures from Africa and the Diaspora.

Minneapolis, MN: Fortress Press, 2010.

Park, Andrew Sung. From Hurt to Healing: A Theology of the Wounded. Nashville, TN: Abingdon Press, 2004.

Peterson, E. H. The Message: The Bible in Contemporary Language. Colorado Springs, CO: NavPress, 2005.

Pitney, David Howard. The African American Jeremiad: Appeals for Justice in America. Philadelphia, PA: Temple University Press, 2005.

Posey, James Anthony. "The Church Without Walls: A New Faith Community Model for Ministry in Urban Residential Settings." DMin diss., United Theological Seminary, 2011.

Powell, John A. Racing to Justice: Transforming Our Conceptions of Self and Other to Build an Inclusive Society. Bloomington, IN: Indiana University Press, 2012. Kindle.

Richards, Lawrence O. The Bible Reader's Companion. Wheaton, IL: Victor Books, 1991. _____. The Teacher's Commentary.

Wheaton, IL: Victor Books, 1987. Ringe, Sharon. Jesus, Liberation, and the Biblical Jubilee. Philadelphia, PA: Fortress Press, 1985.

Salvatierra, Alexia, and Peter Heltzel. FaithRooted Organizing: Mobilizing the Church in

Service to the World. Downers Grove, IL: InterVarsity Press, 2014. Kindle.

Seventh-day Adventist Church. "World Church." Accessed February 4, 2014. http://www.adventist.org/world-church/.

Smith, J. E. The Books of History. Joplin, MO: College Press, 1995.

Smith, Michael Denzel. Invisible Man, Got the Whole World Watching: A Young Black Man's Education. New York, NY: Nation Books, 2016.

Stearns, Richard. The Hole in Our Gospel, Special Edition: What Does God Expect of Us? The Answer That Changed My Life and Might Just Change the World. Nashville, TN: Thomas Nelson, 2014. Kindle.

Stefanovic, Ranko. Plain Revelation: A Reader's Introduction to the Apocalypse. Berrien Springs, MI: Andrews University Press, 2013.

Swanson, J. Dictionary of Biblical Languages with Semantic Domains: Hebrew Old Testament. Oak Harbor, WA: Logos Research Systems, 1997.

Sweet, Leonard. Me and We: God's New Social Gospel. Nashville, TN: Abingdon Press, 2014. Kindle.

Tagert-Paul, Kimberly. "Social Justice, A Christian Duty?" Seventh-day Adventist Church. October 23, 2014. Accessed March 1, 2015. https://www.adventist.org/en/service/religiousliberty/article/go/-/social-justice-a-christian-duty/. Taylor, Keeanga-Yamahtt Taylor. From #BlackLivesMatter to Black Liberation. Chicago, IL:

Haymarket Books, 2016. Telushkin, Joseph. Jewish Literacy. New York, NY: HarperCollins, 2010. Kindle.

Throntveit, Mark A. Ezra-Nehemiah: Interpretation: A Bible Commentary for Teaching and Preaching. Louisville, KY: Westminster John Knox Press, 2012. Kindle.

US Census Bureau. "Census.gov." Accessed February 4, 2014. http://www.census.gov/.

Waetjan, Herman C. A Reordering of Power: A Socio-Political Reading of Mark's Gospel. Eugene, OR: Wip and Stock, 2014.

Walton, John H., Victor H. Matthews, and Mark W. Chavals. The IVP Bible Background Commentary: Old Testament. Downers Grove, IL: Intervarsity Press, 2000.

Warnock, Raphael G. The Divided Mind of the Black Church: Theology, Piety, and Public Witness (Religion, Race, and Ethnicity). New York, NY: NYU Press, 2013. Kindle.

White, Ellen G. The Ministry of Healing. Mountain View, CA: Pacific Press Publishing Association, 1942.

_____. The Southern Work. Indianapolis, IN: Review and Herald Publishing, 2004.

Wiersbe, W. W. Be Determined. Wheaton, IL: Victor Books, 1996.

Wolterstorff, Nicholas. Justice: Rights and Wrongs. Princeton, NJ: Princeton University Press, 2010.

Ziedenberg, Jason, and Vincent Schiraldi. Race and Imprisonment in Texas: The Disparate Incarceration of Latinos and African Americans in the Lone Star State. Justice Policy Institute. 2005.

Accessed February 4, 2014. http://www.justicepolicy.org/images/upload/0502_rep_txraceimprisonment_ac-rd.pdf.

CPSIA information can be obtained
at www.ICGtesting.com
Printed in the USA
FSHW022225200219
55819FS

9 781948 877190